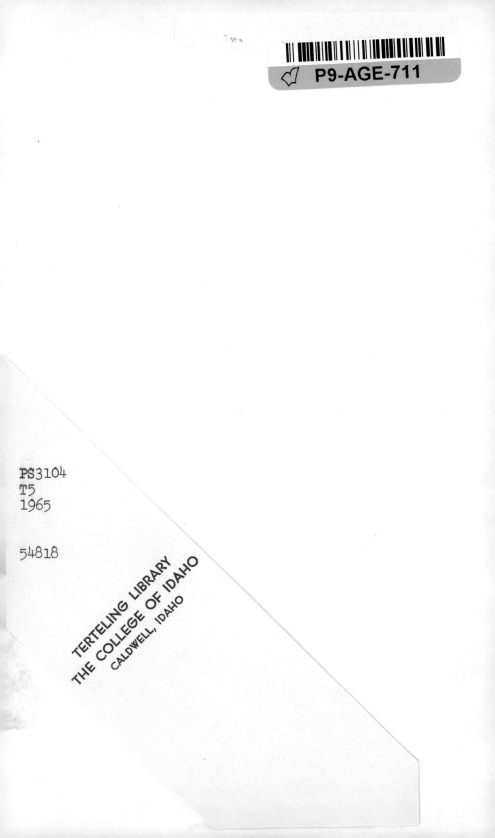

THE COMPLETE POEMS OF
FREDERICK GODDARD TUCKERMAN

*   *   *

The COMPLETE *Poems of*

FREDERICK GODDARD TUCKERMAN

Edited, with an Introduction, by

N. SCOTT MOMADAY

*   *   *   *   *

WITH A CRITICAL FOREWORD BY

YVOR WINTERS

New York

OXFORD UNIVERSITY PRESS

1965

PREFACE

IF THE POEMS of Frederick Goddard Tuckerman are to be considered a real and legitimate part of American literature, we must be willing to search out their historical as well as their literary meaning. I refer, not so much to the explicit, but the *consequent* historical meaning. It seems to me that historical analysis is an indispensable step in the critical process. The critics of Tuckerman's poems will have always to keep before them the poems themselves as the central concern; yet they will have also to look at the intellectual age against which the poems assume so crucial an individuality. It will be necessary to carry on the investigation implied in the foreword and introduction.

I wish to acknowledge the kindness of Professor William A. Jackson, Director of the Houghton Library, in permitting me to examine the Tuckerman manuscripts and to secure them on microfilm.

I wish also to acknowledge the assistance of Mrs. Sarah W. Flannery, Coordinator of the Humanities, Boston Public Library, and Mr. Francis Brown, editor of the *New York Times Book Review*.

For giving generously of his time and attention, I am indebted to Professor David M. Potter of Stanford University.

I am especially indebted to Professor Albert J. Guerard of Stanford for his perceptive criticism of the introduction and appendices at each stage of development and for the sincere interest with which he regarded the textual problems.

On several accounts I give my sincere thanks to Edmund Wilson.

N. S. M.

University of California at Santa Barbara
April 1964

CONTENTS

FOREWORD

F. G. TUCKERMAN (1821-73) was one of the three most remarkable American poets of the nineteenth century. The others were Jones Very (1813-80) and Emily Dickinson (1830-86). Emerson had talent, which was badly damaged by foolish thinking; Bryant might be described as a fine second-rate poet, better than most of the British poets of the century. Of Poe and Whitman, the less said the better. Very was Tuckerman's tutor at Harvard for a brief period, but their connections thereafter seem to have been slight. Tuckerman spent most of his mature life within about eighteen miles of Amherst, but there is no evidence that he or Emily Dickinson ever met or even knew of each other's existence. Miss Dickinson knew Tuckerman's son and probably knew his brother the Amherst botanist, a specialist in mosses, and the distinguished member of the family (a ravine was named after him).

All three of these poets were isolated personally (I suspect as a result of boredom). They were isolated from each other by their methods and attitudes. Very was a Calvinist mystic who wrote a few fine poems but repeated and diluted himself to almost infinite tedium. Miss Dickinson came from a Calvinistic background, but she appears quite obviously never to have experienced the conversion which she deeply desired: the matter of her best poems is the honest and intelligent appraisal of an impossible situation. She was a country girl with exasperating mannerisms; but her natural genius was great, and she wrote a few great poems. Tuckerman's religious background appears to have been Episcopalian, but there are only a few poems which exhibit any explicitly religious interest, the important one being Sonnet XXVIII of the first series ("Not the round natural world").

It is not Tuckerman's relationship to New England poetry which interests me, however; it is his relationship to the romantic and post-romantic poetry in English and in French as we see this poetry in the nineteenth and twentieth centuries. If we confine our attention to the sonnets, we find a kind of chronic melancholy, which for the most part appears to be an indulgence. The death of his wife gave Tuckerman a legitimate cause for melancholy, but the condition seems to have preceded her death, and even after her death it continues, without, except in a few poems, any explicit justification. There is also a consistent interest, not necessarily romantic in itself, but common in romantic poetry, in the description of natural detail. In such description he surpasses the British romantics except, perhaps, for an occasional line or short passage in Wordsworth. Wordsworth, the poet of nature, popularized nature but almost never saw it: his descriptions are almost always stereotypes. Tuckerman very often saw it. He used his perceptions of nature in various ways.

Sonnet XVI of the second series describes the deserted home of Gertrude and Gulielma, the deceased sisters, who seem to haunt several of the sonnets. The first four lines are excellent, the next three respectable; the eighth again is excellent. The ninth is as good as the first four; the tenth is a sentimental stereotype. In the last five lines, we have one of the most beautiful descriptions in nineteenth-century poetry, but marred again by the second of these lines:

> The wild rain enters, and the sunset wind
> Sighs in the chambers of their loveliness
> Or shakes the pane—and in the silent noons
> The glass falls from the window, part by part,
> And ringeth faintly in the grassy stones.

The faults of the sonnet are those of the nineteenth century; the fine lines are of a kind which the nineteenth-century poets are often thought to exhibit but of which they are seldom capable. Most readers today regard the bad writing of the nineteenth century (as we find it, for example, almost everywhere in Keats and Wordsworth) as great writing; when such writing occurs in later poets, such as Bridges (and we can find a good deal of it in his inferior work), it is regarded as a vice, and it serves to obscure the virtues of such poets. I fear that such lines may obscure the virtues of Tuckerman, for, although he is definitely of the nineteenth century, he has emerged more or less recently in our own century. Bad lines, of course (like bad poems), are always bad, but we should not allow them to obscure the extent to which a poet has emerged from an unfortunate context.

But what is the context? It is certainly that of the nineteenth century, but the sensibility of this sonnet and of many others is not that of England or of New England in Tuckerman's time. If one seeks an English poet resembling Tuckerman one will scarcely find him, except in so far as Tuckerman imitates (not too badly) Wordsworth and Tennyson in some of his early, longer, and inferior pieces. If one seeks a New England poet, I can think of no one save Frost in a few of his short lyrics ("Spring Pools," perhaps), but Tuckerman had not read Frost, and Frost had almost certainly not read Tuckerman at so early a date. The landscape in the sonnets is that of New England, but the sensibility is that of the gentler French symbolism, that of Verlaine in particular; yet the French poets had not read Tuckerman, and it seems inconceivable that he had read any of them. One can only say that these things happen.

I will quote the first stanza of the fifth poem in Verlaine's "Romances sans Paroles":

> Le piano que baise une main frêle
> Luit dans le soir rose et gris vaguement,
> Tandis qu'avec un très léger bruit d'aile
> Un air bien vieux, bien faible et bien charmant,
> Rôde discret, épeuré quasiment,
> Par le boudoir longtemps parfumé d'Elle.

This stanza in its way might pass as a mere expansion of the second line from Tuckerman in the passage which I have quoted. The scene is different, but the theme and the facile sentiment are the same; and in each there is the same sensibility. Verlaine, however, controls this particular tone more successfully throughout his poem, and in this respect his poem is more successful than Tuckerman's. The interesting fact about Tuckerman's line is this: it is a falling-off from the main body of the poem and so appears defective. Both poems are gentle elegies, and both are minor poems; but the best detail in Tuckerman's poem is better than anything in Verlaine's, and the poem is more moving than Verlaine's.

Sonnet XVIII of the same group is perhaps more uniformly successful, and the last six lines are the most powerful in the sonnets:

> Here, but a lifetime back, where falls tonight
> Behind the curtained pane a sheltered light
> On buds of rose or vase of violet
> Aloft upon the marble mantel set,
> Here in the forest-heart, hung blackening
> The wolfbait on the bush beside the spring.

The poem compares the back country of the poet's time with the same country sixty or seventy years before; the present scene is dominated by the past; the last two lines are appalling in their darkness and solitude. And yet they may be more than this: Mr. Momaday assures me that they may also be nostalgic, and he could be right. Neither one of us is a New Englander, but I trust his judgment here farther than my own. The last two lines above take us rather far from Verlaine, in any event; but the sharp perception of detail is still there.

Sonnet X of the first series is one of the strangest and at the same time one of the most beautiful. It deals with a man of whom we know nothing except that he is obsessed with terror and anguish. The man may be an imaginative projection of the poet or he may be some other man. We know nothing of the reasons for his condition; he is as purely romantic as something out of Poe, at least when we consider the bare conception of the poem. But Tuckerman's genius emerges in a line as remarkable as this:

> I cannot rid the thought nor hold it close . . .

and in the beautiful descriptive lines below:

> The cricket chides beneath the doorstep stone
> And greener than the season grows the grass.

And then there is the obscure conclusion:

> Nor can I drop my lids nor shade my brows,
> But there he stands beside the lifted sash;
> And with a swooning of the heart, I think
> Where the black shingles slope to meet the boughs

And, shattered on the roof like smallest snows,
The tiny petals of the mountain ash.

There have been a few occasions when I almost thought that I understood the grammar and syntax of this passage, but I do not understand them now. I understand the general intention: somehow the sensory details express the sickness of the man; the tiny details are the items on which he can concentrate; but that is all we know.

One can observe the same thing in a more vigorous poem, "Larme," by Rimbaud. It is a progression into pure obscurity. The French symbolists had a theory for this: one finds it in the prose and many of the late sonnets of Mallarmé, in "Art Poétique" by Verlaine, and in "Bonheur" by Rimbaud. There is no such theory in Tuckerman; he merely slipped into it. The French tradition came out of it in the two great poems by Valéry, "Le Cimetière Marin" and "Ébauche d'un serpent," written early in our century, and came out of it without benefit of much in the way of theory. Tuckerman, who had slipped into it without theory, came out of it without theory in his great poem *The Cricket*, written in his last years. Briefly, what happened is this: there was an acute sharpening of sensory perception in the romantic movement, mainly in the late nineteenth century in France and in the early twentieth century in the United States, a sharpening taken so seriously as an end in itself that it led to confusion. This sharpening seems to have occurred briefly in the third quarter of the nineteenth century in a village in western Massachusetts, in the work of F. G. Tuckerman. The form of the emergence is as follows: the acute sensory perception remains; but instead of the simple elegiac theme which we get in some of Verlaine and much of Heredia, and in the first two sonnets by Tuckerman from which I have quoted, instead of the obscure emotionalism of much of Verlaine and Rimbaud and of the last lines which I have quoted from Tuckerman, we have a theme of some intellectual scope with enough abstract statement to support the theme; theme and abstract statement charge the imagery with meaning, with the result that the imagery has the force of abstract statement. The imagery is not ornament as in much of the poetry of the Renaissance, nor is it merely the pasturage for revery as in much of the poetry of the eighteenth, nineteenth, and twentieth centuries. The structure is that of controlled association. The two great poems by Valéry and "Sunday Morning" by Stevens (perhaps a year or two earlier than the first of the two French poems) will serve as examples. *The Cricket* is a greater poem than "Sunday Morning" and is almost equal to either of the poems by Valéry.

The Cricket is composed of five sections; the riming is irregular and the lines vary in length; the meter is iambic. The poem belongs in the tradition of the "great odes," of which "Alexander's Feast" by Dryden is the first well-known example, although "Lycidas" might be regarded as a precursor, for its principles are similar and its influence on later examples is obvious: these poems dealt with what purported to be an important subject, were of some length, and were associational in structure and in the use of imagery (and often loosely associational). Most of the odes of Gray (including the "Elegy"), of Collins, Keats, Wordsworth, Tennyson, and others fall in this category. These poems suggest the structure of *The Cricket,* although the structure of Tuckerman's poem is far more controlled than is the structure of most of these. Tuckerman's poem has a background in English poetry of which he was probably conscious. As to its resemblances with later French and American poetry, he was obviously ignorant, and the French and American poets were obviously ignorant of him.

The first section is a quiet and affectionate invocation to the cricket merely as a cricket. The adjective "cooing" at the end of this section disturbs some readers. The singular number in this line is collective in effect: we have the confused sound of crickets. We have the crickets as familiar, almost domestic, creatures; but, in the light of what follows, the gentle and almost sentimental effect of the adjective becomes quietly ironic. In the second section we meet the cricket in multiplicity spread throughout a summer landscape, in which the heat, scent, and sound are hypnotic and stun the sense to slumber; we approach a pantheistic trance; and at the end of the passage the sound of the crickets is compared to the sound of the sea. The sea is a traditional symbol of the changing physical universe from which we arise and to which we return, and it is often in addition a symbol of those elements in human nature which elude understanding and control, and which may be destructive. In the third section we are told that the cricket is dear to the child and is a lover of night, and this carries us further into the nostalgia for the primitive, the sub-human. The sea recurs in this connection, and, although the lines describing it are the weakest in the poem, they are related to the theme. This brings us to death and the grave and some of the greatest lines in the poem:

> With faces where but now a gap must be,
> Renunciations, and partitions deep
> And perfect tears, and crowning vacancy!

and the two final lines of the section. In the fourth section the cricket and his relatives are projected into primitive antiquity. The procedure has been associational, but the association has been controlled: the cricket has become a symbol for non-human nature and for the primitive and sub-human in human nature and has been used to create a deep longing for these qualities and for death.

The fifth section draws all of these elements together into a final statement and contains the greatest writing in the poem. The poet longs to resemble the old enchanter who employed *evil* drugs to learn the languages of the lower creatures. He would thus be unwise, would descend through denser stillness, would convert the world to the cricket's wisdom, would gain the low applause of the sub-human world, would possess a great deal, but would yield more. He then recognizes the impossibility of this choice, and accepts the necessity of living at the human level until the end of his life. The conclusion is similar to that of "Le Cimetière Marin." The philosophic ideas of Valéry are not those of Tuckerman, but the two poems bear a striking resemblance not merely in the conclusions but in the quality of the imagery. The poem resembles Ben Jonson's "To Heaven," in this respect: it is a poem dealing with the sin of despair, of the desire for death. But it is a poem written in a later period, with a different set of ideas and a different sensibility. The sensibility is related to that of Valéry.

The theme has been sufficiently established in conceptual terms; it permeates the imagery. The imagery, as it occurs, has no need of explanation, and it is not ornamental; the thought of the poem exists in the imagery and develops through it. The imagery is magnificent in its own right:

> Might I but find thy knowledge in thy song!
>   That twittering tongue,
> Ancient as light, returning like the years.

There is the marvelous command of cadence, sometimes in the use of the short lines:

> Content to bring thy wisdom to the world;
> Content to gain at last some low applause,
>   Now low, now lost . . .

We continue with the idea of the infinitely numerous but sub-human audience in the realm of temptation and with the non-human realm of the purely physical, worlds in spite of which the poet must somehow survive:

> For larger would be less indeed, and like
> The ceaseless simmer in the summer grass
> To him who toileth in the windy field,
>   Or where the sunbeams strike,
> Naught in innumerable numerousness.
>   So might I much possess,
>   So much must yield;

The poem proceeds from here to the solution which I have mentioned; and in the final lines we have one of the greatest passages in our poetry:

>   Behold! the autumn goes,
>   The shadow grows,
> The moments take hold of eternity;

Tuckerman is flawed by the vices of his century; but *The Cricket*, I feel sure, is the greatest poem in English of the century, and the amount of unforgettable poetry in the sonnets is large. The most curious fact, so far as I am concerned, is the development through the poetic modes which I have discussed—a development which did not occur in England at all, and which in France required about three generations. In Tuckerman's work it occurred in the lifetime (not a long one) of one man, in Greenfield, Massachusetts, and without benefit of models.

Yvor Winters

INTRODUCTION

EDMUND WILSON states that "Tuckerman has emerged at last from the obscurity which the retirement of his life invited."[1] It would be more accurate to say that Tuckerman's emergence has begun; certainly it is not complete. The beginning has a history of more than fifty years.

Shortly after the turn of the century, a Mr. Louis How of New York set about compiling an anthology of American poems. The work did not come to publication, but it caught the attention of Walter Prichard Eaton, the drama critic and essayist. Included in the manuscript were two sonnets by Frederick Goddard Tuckerman. Having seen them, Eaton became interested in the man who wrote them, and he sought out Tuckerman's published poems. These were contained in a single volume, the last printing of which occurred in 1869. Eaton then wrote an article about Tuckerman and his poems which appeared in the January issue of *Forum*, 1909. Eaton's essay initiated the emergence of which Edmund Wilson speaks. It was seen by Witter Bynner, who then entered into correspondence with the poet's granddaughter, Margaret Tuckerman Clark of Amherst, now deceased. Bynner discovered, in Mrs. Clark's keeping, the unpublished poems. In 1931 he brought out his edition of the sonnets.

Frederick Goddard Tuckerman was a lifelong resident of Massachusetts. He was born February 4, 1821, in Boston, and he died May 9, 1873, in Greenfield. The essential facts of his life are contained in Bayard Tuckerman's genealogy, *Notes on the Tuckerman Family*, privately printed in Boston in 1914.

Frederick G. Tuckerman, born in Boston, February 4, 1821, prepared for college at the private school of Bishop Hopkins[2] and at the Boston

---

[1] Edmund Wilson, *Patriotic Gore* (New York, 1962), 490.
[2] John Henry Hopkins, first Protestant Episcopal bishop of Vermont and

Latin School, and entered Harvard with the class of 1841. But serious trouble with his eyes, from which he never fully recovered, forced him to leave college. Later, he entered the law school, graduating in 1842, and was admitted to the Suffolk Bar. Finding the practice of law distasteful, he abandoned it and devoted himself to the pursuit of his favorite studies—literature, botany, and astronomy. His love of nature led him in early manhood to settle in the country. He had a fine telescope, and for several years kept a journal of astronomical and meteorological phenomena, from time to time publishing his observations. As a botanist he was recognized as an authority on the Flora of Franklin County and the adjacent region. He travelled abroad twice. During his second visit, in 1855, he was the guest of Alfred Tennyson at Farringford, Isle of Wight, who gave him the original manuscript of *Locksley Hall*, now in the possession of his son. Poems by him appeared in the *Living Age*, *Putnam's* and *Atlantic* magazines. In 1860 they were collected and privately printed, and afterwards published in Boston and London.

He married, June 17, 1847, Hannah L., daughter of David S. Jones, of Greenfield, Massachusetts, and had three children: Edward, the fifth and last of the name, who died in his twenty-first year; a daughter Anna; and a son Frederick.[3]

Edward Tuckerman, the poet's father, was a partner in the Boston firm of Tuckerman, Rogers and Cushing, Wholesalers and Importers. He died in 1842, leaving an ample inheritance. His second wife, Sophia, bore him three sons and a daughter. The eldest son, whose name was Edward also, became an eminent botanist and was for many years on the faculty of Amherst College. The second son, Samuel, gained an important reputation both in America and Europe as a musicologist. The youngest of the

rector of St. Paul's Church in Burlington. It is not surprising that Edward Tuckerman should send his son to an Episcopal bishop for an education; he was himself a vestryman of St. Paul's in Boston and a trustee of the Massachusetts Episcopal Theological School. He was converted to Unitarianism in 1796. Successively he became a member of the Hollis and Federal Street Churches. He also attended the New North Church where his brother-in-law, Dr. Francis Parkman, was minister. He returned to the Episcopal Church not earlier than 1813. See Samuel A. Golden, *Frederick Goddard Tuckerman: An American Sonneteer* (University of Maine Studies, Second Series, No. 66, April, 1952), 2, 8.

[3] Hannah Lucinda (Jones) Tuckerman died May 12, 1857, five days after the birth of her third child, Frederick. Her firstborn was Edward (1848-69); her daughter was Anna (1853-?). Frederick died in 1929.

children was, like her mother, named Sophia, and, like her brother Frederick, she cultivated an interest in literature by writing.

The youngest son was named for F. W. Goddard, a kinsman who traveled with William Wordsworth in Switzerland in 1820, and whose accidental death while crossing the Lake of Zurich was the subject of an elegy by Wordsworth. As a boy and a young man, Frederick Goddard Tuckerman lived at Boston in a house on Beacon Street. In 1847, he removed to Greenfield, in western Massachusetts. The life he began at Greenfield was a strange one for a man in his middle twenties; it was a life of relative seclusion and retirement. He married in the same year Hannah Lucinda Jones, a dark-haired, gentle woman, whose disposition was well suited to his own. Ten years later Hannah died, within a week after the birth of her third child. Her death was the deepest hurt of Tuckerman's life and the beginning of his final solitude.

In 1851, and again in 1854, Tuckerman journeyed abroad. On the first of these excursions he met Alfred Tennyson; on the second he was Tennyson's guest at Farringford. The friendship between the two men appears to have been fast and of long standing. We do not know what Tennyson thought of Tuckerman's poetry. It is not unlikely that he read the manuscript dated 1854, from which the 1860 edition of the *Poems* was printed. In 1863, a second edition was published in London with slight revision.[4] Bynner speculates that the English publication "may have been the result of Tennyson's interest."

The American writers to whom Tuckerman sent complimentary copies of the 1860 *Poems* are an impressive lot. The list of recipients includes the names of Emerson, Hawthorne, Longfellow, Bryant, and Jones Very. Tuckerman anxiously awaited acknowledgment; he even inquired of Hawthorne in advance whether or not his gift would be acceptable. This was Tuckerman's way of insuring himself against disappointment; it is the way of a mild, sensi-

---

[4] The issues of 1863, 1864, and 1869 are identical texts. The difference between the 1860 and 1863 editions is slight. Two sets of plates only were used in the printing of all four volumes. Golden erroneously states that "The Ticknor and Fields 1864 edition is exactly the same as the privately printed edition with the exception of division of contents into Part I and Part II." (Golden, *op. cit.*, 31). In the two poems "The School Girl: an Idyll" and "Sidney" there are textual differences as well. See Appendix I.

tive man. When Hawthorne had seen the book he sent to Tuckerman the following letter:

Concord
April 14, 1861

My Dear Sir,—

I have read the volume of poems and think it a remarkable one. . . . I question whether the poems will obtain a very early or wide acceptance from the public either in England or America because their merit does not lie upon the surface, but must be looked for with faith and sympathy, and a kind of insight as when you look into a carbuncle to discover its hidden fire.

The second reading does more for them than the first, and I have no doubt many of them will glow brighter and brighter on reflected perusal. "The Stranger" impressed me a good deal, so did "Picomegan" and "Margites"; and the whole series of sonnets; although I might have liked other pieces as well, if I had made myself equally familiar with them. The greatest difficulty with you will be to get yourself read at all; if you could be read twice, the book might be a success. . . .

Sincerely yours,
Nath Hawthorne

Earlier by just more than two weeks, Tuckerman received the following letter from Ralph Waldo Emerson.

Concord, 28 March, 1861

My Dear Sir:

My best thanks for the Book you have sent me. It has given me great pleasure,—more than I dared hope for in opening it. I think "Rhotruda" a perfect success in its kind; and it should be bound up as a fifth in your friend Tennyson's "Idyls," as Chapman finished Marlow's "Hero and Leander." After this I like "Mark Atherton," "The Stranger," "The Schoolgirl," and "Elidore." And I see well the love of native flowers, the skill to name them and delight in words that are melodies, which have given you first and then your reader so much content.

The presumption against a poetic success is so immense that to have written one poem seems worth living for. I advised Fields the publisher on Saturday to entreat you to print "Rhotruda" in the *Atlantic*. I am quite sure you will presently publish the book, or a large part of it. If you do not your readers will; and, in the interval, I hope you will give the *Atlantic* the privilege of announcing this poem, the arrival of what is so rich and rare. I have much to say about this book, and when we ride again in a train together, I hope you will give me the chance to say it. Meantime I remain your happy debtor.

R. W. Emerson[5]

"If you care to know my opinion of them," wrote Henry Wadsworth Longfellow of the *Poems* in a letter dated April 5, 1861, "I will say that it is very favorable." Then, much like Hawthorne, Longfellow went on to distinguish between the intrinsic merit of Tuckerman's work and "external success":

They are thoughtful and full of feeling; and breathe an air of the country, an odor of farms, which is healthy and suggestive of strength. You have my best thanks for your remembrance of me, and my best wishes for the success of your volume. I mean its external success with the world, which is something quite apart from its internal success, as an expression of your own thoughts and feelings.

The printing of Tuckerman's volume of poems in 1860 was the high point of his public career. When he had made his claim on the attention of the most respected literary men of his day, he returned to his seclusion. He continued to write; indeed, the best of his work was yet to come, but he never again exposed himself to the world. He seems scarcely to have taken notice when Ticknor and Fields brought out the American issue of the *Poems* in 1864. The last of his sonnets was written in 1872. By then he was obscure in our literature, and the following year he was dead.

Frederick G. Tuckerman died Friday evening of disease of the heart, at his boarding place, the American House, aged 52 years. He was a graduate of Harvard and of the Law School, and though admitted to the bar, never practiced his profession. Possessed of ample fortune from the estate of his father, Edward Tuckerman, a highly successful Boston merchant, he lived a retired and secluded life among us. He was an excellent scholar, and has published several fine

5 "Rhotruda" was printed in *The Atlantic Monthly* of July, 1861. Obviously Emerson and Tuckerman were not strangers to each other. Nothing is known of the implication that the two men had met or been on a train together.

poems. His wife was the daughter of David S. Jones, late of Greenfield. She died many years ago.

This was his obituary in the *Greenfield Gazette*. The world, which had already passed him by, paused for a moment to reckon who he was. It was as if Tuckerman had himself died "many years ago."

*   *   *

"Never did a man write poetry more straightly to himself," observed Bynner, "with nothing fictitious. He is isolated in an intense integrity toward nature . . ." That is more than an incidental truth; it is an important statement about nineteenth-century American literature. The terms *isolated, integrity* and *nature* are particularly meaningful in the intellectual and literary history of the Middle Period.

Tuckerman's isolation is complex. It is physical as well as psychological, moral as well as intellectual. Bynner speaks of an isolation that is, in essence, a kind of honesty. Edmund Wilson observes that Tuckerman is a "dissociated" poet and an inventor of mythologies. And the writer for the *Greenfield Gazette* reports simply that Tuckerman "lived a retired and secluded life among us." In order to understand Tuckerman's isolation, it is necessary to bear in mind the special importance which Americans placed upon the idea of self-reliance in the nineteenth century. Although economic collectivism had begun with the experiment of the plantations in the South and industrial capitalism in the North, the concept of the free individual was more fundamental to the Republic than either the farm or the factory. A condition of isolation, which in the seventeenth and eighteenth centuries had been a hard necessity, was in the nineteenth a matter of pride and principle. In Tuckerman's New England, the idea of the free individual arose in part from a change in religious attitudes. As the wilderness receded, Calvinism declined. The faith of the first generations in New England was peculiarly an instrument of survival, for it taught nothing so well as vigilance; but it also bred suspicion and fear and was so closely defined as to be inflexible. After Yorktown, the old Genevan precepts seemed far indeed from the burgeoning realities of national eminence and personal opportunity. The visible expansion of the frontier, reaching outward for self-containment, was a metaphor in which the concept of the free individual —and the principle of isolation—might find expression even in the land itself. It is this metaphor which lies behind Bynner's statement and illuminates in particular the question of integrity. Tuckerman's integrity consists in an absolute dedication to the use and value of reason in the world of matter. In our own age of scientific revolution, it is possible to judge the meaning of Tuckerman's commitment only with reference to the context of American Romanticism.

The chief spokesman of the nineteenth-century New England mind was Ralph Waldo Emerson. Again and again he preached that nature is the vital force of the universe, the absolute unity of all being. He called that unity the "Over-Soul" and promulgated the philosophy of the One. He was suspicious of division. His mind grasped wholes and passed over fragments without patience. He believed science to be invalid; it was committed to the piecemeal investigation of a divisible world. "When I behold a rich landscape," he wrote, "it is less to my purpose to recite correctly the order and superposition of the strata than to know why all thought of multitude is lost in a tranquil sense of unity." Emerson looked at nature through a veil of tradition and morality. What he saw was not the material world, but a gigantic symbol of the abstract "Over-Soul." "Things admit of being used as symbols," he said, "because nature is a symbol, in the whole, and in every part. Every line we can draw in the sand has expression; and there is no body without its spirit of genius."

Frederick Goddard Tuckerman was neither a preacher nor a philosopher, but he was a scientist by avocation. He was at home in the sciences of botany and astronomy, and he knew more than most men about geology. He could look with inexhaustible patience at the particles of nature, and he could call them by name. He was not a pantheist, nor did he incline toward pantheism. He was not a mystic, nor did he recommend the mystical experience. Tuckerman and Emerson were at odds on the most fundamental points.

In order to understand these differences clearly, it will be useful to enumerate and compare with Tuckerman's views the principal aesthetic implications of the Emersonian philosophy. In the first section of his essay entitled *Nature*, Emerson outlined several tenets of a particular Romantic theory. They are as follows:

1. Solitude is more desirable than society. Emerson recommends solitude explicitly. Tuckerman may be said to recommend solitude implicitly and by example.

2. The landscape is a barometer of moral change. This premise, perhaps more than any other, distinguishes the Emersonian ideal. It is current and widespread in our literature. "Nature always wears the colors of the spirit," wrote Emerson. "To a man laboring under calamity, the heat of his own fire hath sadness in it. Then there is a kind of contempt of the landscape felt by him who has just lost by death a dear friend. The sky is less grand as it shuts down over less worth in the population." The first and last sentences of this statement are not merely figurative; Emerson believed them to be literally true. "The Universe is the externization of the soul," he declared; ". . . every thing in nature answers to a moral power . . ." There is in this context a crucial difference between Emerson and Tuckerman. Tuckerman was a keen student of the natural world. He perceived in much greater detail than did Emerson the shape and texture of his surroundings, and he was therefore able to cull and describe those details of setting which so complement the emotional content of his poems. But he attributed no moral significance to the details themselves. Unlike Emerson, he perceived that the determination of "worth in the population" requires a moral judgment which the landscape, no matter how the intelligence views it, cannot reflect.

3. Intuition is superior to intellection. The Emersonian thesis is clear: communion with nature is possible only through the repudiation of reason. But the repudiation of reason is also the rejection of maturity. "The lover of nature is he . . . who has retained the spirit of infancy even into the era of manhood," said Emerson. Thus realized in solitude, verified by its own reflection in nature, and received in "the spirit of infancy," the Emersonian Romantic experience verges on the mystical:

. . . Crossing a bare common, in snow puddles, at twilight, under a clouded sky, without having in my thoughts any occurrence of special good fortune, I am glad to the brink of fear. In the woods, too, a man casts off his years, as the snake his slough, and at what period soever of life is always a child. . . . Standing on the bare ground—my head bathed by the blithe air and uplifted into infinite space—all mean egotism vanishes. I become a transparent eyeball; I am nothing; I see all; the currents of the Universal Being circulate through me; I am part or parcel of God.

This passage suggests a thorny problem in aesthetics. The mystical experience is ineffable. It cannot occur per se in literature, but must be validated, rendered objectively, given the aesthetic distance of description by a third person. When it is not so validated, it is sure to result in the kind of unfortunate metaphor exemplified by Emerson's "transparent eyeball."

Tuckerman's departure from the Emersonian intuitive tradition is neither total nor unique; yet his view of nature is noticeably different from that which predominates in the literature of his time and place. Where Emerson found realized in nature the transcendent spirit of the universe, Tuckerman saw only a various and inscrutable mask. "A Soul that out of Nature's Deep" provides a clear expression of Tuckerman's "integrity toward nature." The poem deals with a man who is predisposed to find solace in the beauty and quiet of the woods, but who finds instead an unintelligible warfare. Like Emily Dickinson's "What mystery pervades a well!", the poem ends in an anomaly:

> And who would find out Wisdom's grot
> To make her footsteps his,
> Must learn to look where it is not
> As well as where it is.

Tuckerman appreciates fully the anomalies of the natural world: light and shadow, here and there, appearance and reality. The importance of that appreciation in nineteenth-century American poetry cannot easily be overestimated.

It is against the background of Emersonian Romanticism that Witter Bynner's statement about Tuckerman becomes sharply meaningful. Tuckerman is indeed "isolated in an intense integrity toward nature." Superficially, he preserves the stage properties of contemporary Romantic literature: the spirit of isolation, a dissociation of emotional cause and effect, a preoccupation with nature. But Tuckerman's sense of isolation is defined in terms of intellectual honesty rather than self-reliance; his taste is measured in the fact rather than the celebration of sentiment; his attention is trained upon the surfaces rather than the symbols of his world.

* * *

Tuckerman was a man who made herbariums. He had an eye for the minutest aspects of the world. When he wished to focus upon the veins of a leaf, or to find a metaphor for the appearance of an evergreen spine, he could do so with extraordinary skill. His poems are remarkable, point-blank descriptions of nature; they are filled with small, precise, and whole things: purring bees and vervain spikes, shives and amaryllis, wind flowers and stramony. But Tuckerman has more to recommend him than an eye and a nomenclature. His sensibilities are refined; his sensitivity is acute. His experience is pervaded by an always apparent sense of grief. He knows well the side of Man that is most vulnerable to pain, and he treats of it throughout his work with respect and compassion, often with great power and beauty.

But he was also a poet of the nineteenth century, and one who admired Tennyson above others. There is a good deal of bad writing in Tuckerman, and there are many obscurities. I shall not presume to enumerate the faults; let it suffice to say that they occur for the most part in the longer poems, especially those of narrative character. Often they are marred by a tediousness of expression and an overwrought consistency of mood; "Mark Atherton" and the previously unpublished "Nature and Necessity" are chief examples. As for the obscurities, they are more apparent than real; they are distracting nonetheless. There are several names in Tuckerman's poems which have frustrated a good many honest attempts on the part of scholars to document them. Tuckerman possessed a remarkable knowledge of world literature. He could refer with equanimity to Biblical Deborah, historical Artemisia, and mythological Psamathe; he could also appear to have invented such an improbable name as Dagoraus Whear for the sake of rhyme. Edmund Wilson gives over much of his discussion of Tuckerman in *Patriotic Gore* to the matter of historical and mythological allusion. Since the publication of Wilson's book, and in some measure because of it, most of the obscure names in Tuckerman's sonnets have been identified. The three women who are named in the final line of Sonnet XXIV of the first series were the mothers of rulers. Actia is no doubt Atia, the mother of Caesar Augustus, about whom Suetonius tells us:

Eadem Atia, prius quam pareret, somniavit intestina sua ferri ad sidera explicarique per omnem terrarum et caeli ambitum. Somniavit et pater Octavius utero Atiae iubar solis exortum.

Arlotte is Herleve (Arlette) of Falaise, the mother of William the Conqueror. William of Malmesbury records that

Puer ex ea editus, Willelmus a nomine abavi dictus: cujus magnitudinem futuram matris sompnium portendebat, quo intestina sua per totam Normanniam et Angliam extendi et dilatari viderat. . .

and Herodotus tells us that Mandane, the mother of Cyrus the Great, appeared to her father, Astyages, in a dream.

ἐδόκεέ οἱ ἐκ τῶν αἰδοίων τῆς θυγατρός, ταύτης φῦναι
ἄμπελον, τὴν δὲ ἄμπελον ἐπισχεῖν τὴν Ἀσίην πᾶσαν.

The similarity among these passages, even more apparent in the original than in translation, and the precision with which they support the theme of Tuckerman's poem, are indeed noteworthy.

According to Plutarch and others, Epponina (Tuckerman's Eponina of Sonnet XXXVII, second series) was the wife of Julius Sabinus, who joined in Civilis' revolt on the Rhine in A.D. 70. When the revolt failed, Sabinus set fire to his house and took refuge in a cave. It was supposed that he had died in the fire, and he lived in the cave for nine years. Surreptitiously, Epponina visited him and during his long confinement bore him two sons who were presumably kept in hiding with their father. Epponina tried in vain to secure a pardon for her husband. At the end of the nine years, she was executed with him.

The Dagoraus Whear of Sonnet I, third series, is Degory Wheare (1573-1647), the first professor of modern history at Oxford; "his

Method" (line 5) refers to Wheare's Latin dissertation *De Ratione et Methodo Legendi Historias.*

Sonnet VIII of the fifth series contains what appears to be simple licence in the final line,

> With holm tree, ople tree, and sycamine.

Wilson concurs with Bynner in the opinion that Tuckerman is here indulging in a kind of word-play: that ople and sycamine are merely alterations of the words *apple, sycamore,* and *mine,* words which, like *home,* bear connotations peculiarly suited to the nostalgic tone of the poem. In fact, however, holm, ople, and sycamine are the archaic names of real trees. The word *holm* derives from the Anglo-Saxon *holen,* which designated our holly. *Ople* comes from the Latin *opulus* and refers to the guelder-rose or water elder (*Viburnum opulus*), and the *sycamine* is the common black mulberry.

If Tuckerman is to emerge completely in our literature, he had best be revealed for the right reasons. There are two in particular. First, he stands in historical opposition to the mainstream of nineteenth-century American Romanticism. That fact ought now to account for his renown as, for the better part of a century, it has accounted for his anonymity. Tuckerman's intellectual and literary isolation will bear careful investigation, for it constitutes a valid literature in itself. Second, Tuckerman's poems are valuable in their own right. They are the best possessions of a man whose vision is keen and whose judgment is sound.

SONNETS

First Series, 1854-1860

*

KEY TO ABBREVIATIONS

E   Editions of *Poems* by Frederick Goddard Tuckerman, 1860, 1863, 1864, and 1869.

G   Golden, Samuel A. *Frederick Goddard Tuckerman: An American Sonneteer,* 1952.

LA   *Littell's Living Age.*

MS   MS Am 1349: the Tuckerman manuscript.

ORIG: Original word or phrase which Tuckerman changed in manuscript.

P   *Putnam's Magazine.*

S   *The Sonnets of Frederick Goddard Tuckerman,* edited with an introduction by Witter Bynner, 1931.

V   Variant copy of poem in manuscript.

The present edition is based upon Houghton Library MS Am 1349, the Tuckerman manuscripts, for reasons enumerated in Appendix I. For a full account of the manuscripts catalogued under this citation, see Appendix II.

Sometimes, when winding slow by brook and bower,
Beating the idle grass,—of what avail,
I ask, are these dim fancies, cares and fears?
What though from every bank I drew a flower,—
Bloodroot, king orchis, or the pearlwort pale,—
And set it in my verse with thoughtful tears?
What would it count though I should sing my death
And muse and mourn with as poetic breath
As in damp garden walks the autumn gale
Sighs o'er the fallen floriage? What avail
Is the swan's voice if all the hearers fail?
Or his great flight that no eye gathereth
In the blending blue? And yet depending so,
God were not God, whom knowledge cannot know.

II

Wherefore, with this belief held like a blade,
Gathering my strength and purpose still and slow,
I wait, resolved to carry it to the heart
Of that dark doubt in one collected blow,
And stand at guard with spirit undismayed:
Nor fear the Opposer's anger, arms or art,
When from a hiding near behold him start
With a fresh weapon of my weakness made
And goad me with myself, and urge the attack
While I strike short and still give back and back
While the foe rages. Then from that disgrace
He points to where they sit that have won the race,
Laurel on laurel wreathing face o'er face,
And leaves me lower still, for, ranked in place,

When two sonnets appear on a page carets are used to indicate the sonnet
referred to: ∧ upper; ∨ lower.

∨ 2 *still* E and s *fair*　13 *on* E and s *by*　14 *leaves* s *leave*

And borne with theirs, my proudest thoughts do seem
Bald at the best and dim: a barren gleam
Among the immortal stars, and faint and brief
As northlight flitting in the dreary north.
What have thy dreams, a vague prospective worth?
An import imminent? or dost thou deem
Thy life so fair that thou wouldst set it forth
Before the day? or art thou wise in grief,
Has fruitful sorrow swept thee with her wing?
Today I heard a sweet voice carolling
In the woodlot paths, with laugh and careless cry
Leading her happy mates: apart I stepped,
And while the laugh and song went lightly by,
In the wild bushes I sat down and wept.

Nor looks that backward life so bare to me,
My later youth, and ways I've wandered through,
But touched with innocent grace, the purring bee
O'er the maple log, the white-heaped cherry tree
That hummed all day in the sun, the April blue;
Yet hardly now one ray the Forward hath
To show where sorrow rests and rest begins,
Although I check my feet nor walk to wrath
Through days of crime, and grosser shadowings
Of evil done in the dark, but fearfully
Mid unfulfilled yet unrelinquished sins
That hedge me in and press about my path
Like purple-poison flowers of stramony
With their dull opiate breath and dragon wings.

∧ 11 *woodlot* E and s *wood-land*

∨ 3 *purring* E and s *early*   4 *O'er* E and s *On*

V

And so the day drops by, the horizon draws
The fading sun and we stand struck in grief,
Failing to find our haven of relief,
Wide of the way, nor sure to turn or pause,
And weep to view how fast the splendor wanes
And scarcely heed that yet some share remains
Of the red afterlight, some time to mark,
Some space between the sundown and the dark;
But not for him those golden calms succeed
Who while the day is high and glory reigns
Sees it go by, as the dim pampas plain,
Hoary with salt and gray with bitter weed,
Sees the vault blacken, feels the dark wind strain,
Hears the dry thunder roll, and knows no rain.

VI

Not sometimes, but to him that heeds the whole
And in the Ample reads his personal page,
Laboring to reconcile, content, assuage
The vexed conditions of his heritage,
Forever waits an angel at the goal.
And ills seem but as food for spirits sage,
And grief becomes a dark apparelage,
The weed and wearing of the sacred soul.
Might I but count, but here, one watchlight spark!
But vain, O vain this turning for the light,
Vain as a groping hand to rend the dark—
I call, entangled in the night, a night
Of wind and voices, but the gusty roll
Is vague, nor comes their cheer of pilotage.

v 5 *Forever.* Here Bynner and I are faithful to MS. Golden errs in assuming that Bynner ". . . changes 'for ever' to the single word 'forever,' and it is evident that the author's meaning has been obscured.
The 1864 edition reads: 'For ever waits an angel at the goal;' Bynner's version is: 'Forever waits an angel at the goal.' " (G, 42)
In fact, it was not Bynner, but the editor of the *Poems* who separated the parts of the original word. Apparently Golden, in this instance, disregarded MS. 7 *dark* E and s *dim*   14 *their* E and s *there*

VII

Dank fens of cedar, hemlock branches gray
With trees and trail of mosses, wringing-wet,
Beds of the black pitchpine in dead leaves set
Whose wasted red has wasted to white away,
Remnants of rain and droppings of decay,
Why hold ye so my heart, nor dimly let
Through your deep leaves the light of yesterday,
The faded glimmer of a sunshine set?
Is it that in your darkness, shut from strife,
The bread of tears becomes the bread of life?
Far from the roar of day, beneath your boughs
Fresh griefs beat tranquilly, and loves and vows
Grow green in your gray shadows, dearer far
Even than all lovely lights and roses are?

VIII

As when down some broad river dropping, we
Day after day behold the assuming shores
Sink and grow dim, as the great watercourse
Pushes his banks apart and seeks the sea:
Benches of pines, high shelf and balcony,
To flats of willow and low sycamores
Subsiding, till where'er the wave we see,
Himself is his horizon utterly.
So fades the portion of our early world,
Still on the ambit hangs the purple air;
Yet while we lean to read the secret there,
The stream that by green shoresides plashed and purled
Expands: the mountains melt to vapors rare,
And life alone circles out flat and bare.

⋀ 9 *darkness,* E and s *blindness*
⋁ 12 *plashed* E and s *splashed*

[6]

IX

Yet wear we on, the deep light disallowed
That lit our youth; in years no longer young
We wander silently, and brood among
Dead graves, and tease the sunbreak and the cloud
For import: were it not better yet to fly,
To follow those that go before the throng,
Reasoning from stone to star, and easily
Exampling this existence? Or shall I—
Who yield slow reverence where I cannot see
And gather gleams where'er by chance or choice
My footsteps draw, though brokenly dispensed—
Come into light at last? or suddenly
Struck to the knees like Saul, one arm against
The overbearing brightness, hear a voice?

X

An upper chamber in a darkened house,
Where, ere his footsteps reached ripe manhood's brink,
Terror and anguish were his lot to drink;
I cannot rid the thought nor hold it close
But dimly dream upon that man alone:
Now though the autumn clouds most softly pass,
The cricket chides beneath the doorstep stone
And greener than the season grows the grass.
Nor can I drop my lids nor shade my brows,
But there he stands beside the lifted sash;
And with a swooning of the heart, I think
Where the black shingles slope to meet the boughs
And, shattered on the roof like smallest snows,
The tiny petals of the mountain ash.

^ 4 *sunbreak* ORIG:*sungleam*   6 *that* E and S *who*   *throng,* ORIG:*crowd,*
7 *Reasoning* ORIG:*Stepping*   11 *brokenly* MS *falteringly*

v 3 *lot* E and S *cup*   7 *chides* MS *creaks*

[7]

XI

What profits it to me, though here allowed
Life, sunlight, leisure, if they fail to urge
Me to due motion or myself to merge
With the onward stream, too humble, or too proud?
That find myself not with the popular surge
Washed off and on, or up to higher reefs
Flung with the foremost when the rolling crowd
Hoists like a wave, nor strong to speak aloud.
But standing here, gazing on mine own griefs,
Dark household woe, and wounds that bleed and smart,
With still lips and an outcry in the heart,
Or on from day to day I coldly creep
By summer farms and fields, by stream and steep,
Dull, and like one exhausted with deep sleep.

XII

Tall stately plants with spikes and forks of gold
Crowd every slope: my heart repeats its cry,
A cry for strength, for strength and victory:
The will to strive, the courage overbold
That would have moved me once to turn indeed
And level with the dust each lordly weed.
But now I weep upon my wayside walks
And sigh for those fair days, when glorying
I stood a boy amid the mullein-stalks
And wished myself like him the Lion King:
There, where his shield shed arrows and his helm
Rang like a bell beaten with axe and brand,
He pushed the battle backward, realm on realm
Fallen in the swordswing of his stormy hand.

∧ 9 *mine* E and s *my*   10 *Dark* E *Strange*   12 *on* E and s *now,*

∨ 10-14: The diction of the final five lines of both E and s is as follows
(the punctuation is that of s):

And dreamed myself like him the Lion-King.
There, where his shield shed arrows and the clank

[8]

As one who walks and weeps by alien brine
And hears the heavy land-wash break, so I,
Apart from friends, remote in misery,
But brood on pain and find in heaven no sign:
The lights are strange, and bitter voices by.
So the doomed sailor, left alone to die,
Looks sadly seaward at the day's decline
And hears his parting comrades' jeers and scoffs
Or sees through mists that hinder and deform
The dewy stars of home, sees Regulus shine
With a hot flicker through the murky damp
And setting Sirius twitch and twinge like a lamp
Slung to the masthead in a night of storm
Of lonely vessel laboring in the troughs.

XIV

Not proud of station, nor in worldly pelf
Immoderately rich, nor rudely gay:
Gentle he was and generous in a way,
And with a wise direction ruled himself.
Blest Nature spread his table every day,
And so he lived, to all the blasts that woo
Responsible, as yon long locust spray
That waves and washes in the windy blue.
Nor wanted he a power to reach and reap
From hardest things a consequence and use,
And yet this friend of mine, in one small hour
Fell from himself, and was content to weep
For eyes love-dark, red lips, and cheeks in hues
Not red, but rose-dim like the jacinth flower.

Clashed on his helm of battle-axe and brand,
He pushed the battle backward, rank on rank
Fallen in the sword-swing of his stormy hand.

v 5 *Blest* E and s *Large*

And she, her beauty never made her cold,
Young-Oread-like beside the green hill crest
And blissfully obeying Love's behest,
She turned to him as to a god of old,
Her smitten soul with its full strength and spring
Retaliating his love: unto that breast,
Ere scarce the arms dared open to infold,
She gave herself as but a little thing.
And now, to impulse cold, to passion dead,
With the wild grief of unperfected years,
He kissed her hands, her mouth, her hair, her head,
Gathered her close and closer to drink up
The odour of her beauty, then in tears
As for a world, gave from his lips the cup.

Yet Nature, where the thunder leaves its trace
On the high hemlock pine or sandstone bank,
Hating all shock of hue or contrast rank,
With some consenting color heals the place,
Or o'er it draws her mosses green and dank:
So gentle Time will bring with tender craft
Another day, and other greens ingraft
On the dead soil so fire-burned now and blank.
What we have had, we hold, and cannot sink
Remembrance: patience cometh from above;
And now he breathes apart to daily drink
In tears the bitter ashes of his love,
Yet precious rich, and a diviner draught
Than Agria or Artemisia drank.

v 6 *with* s *her*

XVII

All men, the preacher saith, whate'er or whence
Their increase walking through this world has been,
Both those that gather out, or after glean,
Or hold in simple fee of harvests dense,
Though but perhaps a flowerless barren green,
Barren with spots of sorrel, knot grass, spurge:
Yet to one end their differing paths converge
And all must render answer, here or hence.
Lo! Death is at the doors, he crieth, with blows,
But what to him unto whose feverish sense
The stars tick audibly, and the wind's low surge
In the pine, attended, tolls and throngs and grows
On the dread ear, a thunder too profound
For bearing, a Niagara of sound!

XVIII

Perchance his own small field some charge demands:
So full the eternal choral sobs and swells,
But clear away the weeds, although there lurk
Within the weeds a few dim asphodels,
Flowers of a former day, how fair, how fair!
And yet behold them not, but to the work,
Before the short light darken, set thy hands:
Nor over the surface dip with easy share,
But beam-deep, plough and plunge your parallels,
Breaking in clod and flower, that so may spring
From the deep grain a goodlier growth and kind,
Unstirred of heats that blast, of frosts that bind,
Nor swept aside ere the seed catch, by wing
Of casual shower nor any chance of wind.

ʌ 5 *Though* ᴇ and s *Or*   7 *Yet* ᴇ and s *See*

[11]

XIX

Yet vain, perhaps, the fruits our care applaud:
If the Forefate decree the harvest fat
Why should we mind this thing or matter that,
To sift the seed and blow the chaff abroad?
But doubt not so the Giver to defraud
Who will accuse thy labor: spend, nor slack
Of thy best strength and sweetness too, till God
With a full hand and flowing pay thee back.
Behold, on rolling zone and zodiac
The spray and scatter of his bounty flung,
And what canst thou, to whom no hands belong
To hasten by one hour the morning's birth?
Or stay one planet at his circle hung,
In the great flight of stars across the earth?

XX

Still craves the spirit: never Nature solves
That yearning which with her first breath began,
And in its blinder instinct still devolves
On god or pagod, Manada or man,
Or lower yet, brute service, apes and wolves.
By Borneo's surf the bare barbarian
Still to the sands beneath him bows to pray:
Give Greek his god, the Bheel his devil sway
And what remains to me, who count no odds
Between such Lord and him I saw today,
The farmer mounted on his market load,
Bundles of wool and locks of upland hay,
The son of toil that his own works bestrode,
And him, Ophion, earliest of the gods?

v 14 *Ophion.* The name Ophion appears in *Paradise Lost*, Book X, line
581. This is almost certainly Tuckerman's source.

XXI

O Father, God! to whom in happier days
My father bade me cry when troubles fall,
Again I come before thy tribunal
Too faint for prayer and all too blind for praise,
Yet owning never through life's dim career
The eye that would not see and reckless ear:
Against my head no more thy tempests call;
Refreshing that wild sorrow of the heart
And those fierce tears, another morning raise
Upon this vision now so dimmed and swoln:
Guide me as once unto thy feet to flee
Claiming no price of labor, place, or part,
And only seek before thy footstool fall'n
Tears in mine eyes, to lift these hands of me.

XXII

The morning comes, not slow with reddening gold,
But wildly driven with windy shower and sway
As if the wind would blow the dark away:
Voices of wail, of misery multifold,
Wake with the light and its harsh glare obey.
And yet I walk betimes this day of spring,
Still my own private portion reckoning,
Not to compute, though every tear be told.
O might I on the gale my sorrow fling!
But sweep, sweep on, wild blast; who bids thee stay?
Across the stormy headlands shriek and sing
And, earlier than the daytime bring the day
To pouring eyes half-quenched with watery sight,
And breaking hearts that hate the morning light.

v 3 *if* E and s *though*

Shall I not see her? yes: for one has seen
Her in her beauty since we called her dead,
One like herself, a fair young mother led
By her own lot to feel compassion keen;
And unto her last night my Anna came
And sat within her arms and spoke her name
While the old smile, she said, like starlight gleamed,
And like herself in fair young bloom, she said,
Only the white more white, the red more red,
And fainter than the mist her pressure seemed.
And words there were, though vague yet beautiful,
Which she who heard them could not tell to me;
It is enough: my Anna did not flee
To grief or fear, nor lies in slumber dull.

XXIV

Perhaps a dream: yet surely truth has beamed
Oft from the gate of dreams upon the brain
As on yon mountain dark with thunder-rain;
Today through cloudy clefts the glory streamed.
Why do men doubt, and balance, and disdain
Where she, the gentler spirit, seeks to skim
Light from the vague, though thick the shadows swim,
Still counting what she may not all explain—
Not to be lost, or lightly disesteemed
Though cloudy of shape it seem, and meaning dim?
Did Manoah's wife doubt ere she showed to him
The angel standing in the golden grain?
Had Deborah fear? or was that vision vain
That Actia, Arlotte, and Mandané dreamed?

v 3 *dark* E and s *black*

XXV

By this low fire I often sit to woo
Memory to bring the days forever done,
And call the mountains where our love begun
And the dear happy woodlands dipped in dew,
And pore upon the landscape like a book
But cannot find her: or there rise to me
Gardens and groves in light and shadow outspread;
Or on a headland far away I see
Men marching slow in orderly review,
And bayonets flash as, wheeling from the sun,
Rank after rank give fire: or sad, I look
On miles of moonlit brine, with many a bed
Of wave weed heaving. There the wet sands shine
And just awash, the low reef lifts its line.

XXVI

For Nature daily through her grand design
Breathes contradiction where she seems most clear,
For I have held of her the gift to hear
And felt indeed endowed of sense divine
When I have found by guarded insight fine,
Cold April flowers in the green end of June,
And thought myself possessed of Nature's ear
When by the lonely mill-brook into mine,
Seated on slab or trunk asunder sawn,
The night-hawk blew his horn at summer noon;
And in the rainy midnight I have heard
The ground sparrow's long twitter from the pine,
And the catbird's silver song, the wakeful bird
That to the lighted window sings for dawn.

v 8 *into* s *unto*   1o *summer* E and s *sunny*

So to the mind long brooding but on it
A haunting theme for anger, joy, or tears,
With ardent eyes, not what we think appears;
But hunted home, behold! its opposite.
Worn sorrow breaking in disastrous mirth,
And wild tears wept of laughter, like the drops
Shook by the trampling thunder to the earth;
And each seems either, or but a counterfeit
Of that it would dissemble: hopes are fears
And love is woe: nor here the discord stops;
But through all human life runs the account,
Born into pain and ending bitterly—
Yet sweet perchance, betweentime, like a fount
That rises salt and freshens to the sea.

Not the round natural world, not the deep mind,
The reconcilement holds: the blue abyss
Collects it not; our arrows sink amiss
And but in Him may we our import find.
The agony to know, the grief, the bliss
Of toil, is vain and vain: clots of the sod
Gathered in heat and haste and flung behind
To blind ourselves and others, what but this
Still grasping dust and sowing toward the wind?
No more thy meaning seek, thine anguish plead,
But leaving straining thought and stammering word,
Across the barren azure pass to God:
Shooting the void in silence like a bird,
A bird that shuts his wings for better speed.

ᴧ 6 *And wild* s *And with wild*

SONNETS

Second Series, 1854-1860

*

I

That boy, the farmer said, with hazel wand
Pointing him out, half by the haycock hid,
Though bare sixteen, can work at what he's bid
From sun till set, to cradle, reap, or band.
I heard the words, but scarce could understand
Whether they claimed a smile or gave me pain:
Or was it aught to me, in that green lane,
That all day yesterday, the briars amid,
He held the plough against the jarring land
Steady, or kept his place among the mowers
Whilst other fingers, sweeping for the flowers,
Brought from the forest back a crimson stain?
Was it a thorn that touched the flesh, or did
The pokeberry spit purple on my hand?

II

Nor idle all, though naught he sees in thine
But dallying with the day to make it brief
And thinks it braver far to tramp the leaf
With dog and gun, through tamerac, birch, and pine
Or lounge the day beneath a tavern sign:
Yet in *his* labor can I well discern
Great workings moving, both in his and mine.
What though indeed a joyless verse I turn,
The flowers are fair, and give their glistening heaps
To grace her grave: and so tonight I pass
To that low mound gone over now with grass
And find her stirless still, whilst overhead
Creation moveth, and the farmboy sleeps,
A still strong sleep till but the east is red.

∧ 13 *touched* ORIG:*tapped*

∨ 8 *joyless* ORIG:*thankless*   9 *glistening* E and s *glimmering*   10 *grave:*
and E *and* s *rest. And*

[19]

III

Yes, though the brine may from the desert deep
Run itself sweet before it finds the foam,
O what to him, whose deep heart once a home
For love and light, is left? to walk and weep:
Still, with astonished sorrow, watch to keep
On his dead day. He weeps and knows his doom,
Yet standeth stunned; as one who climbs a steep
And, dreaming softly of the cottage room,
The faces round the porch, the rose in showers,
Gains the last height between his heart and it—
And from the windows where his children sleep
Sees the red fire fork or, later come,
Finds, where he left his home, a smouldering pit,
Blackness and scalding stench, for love and flowers.

IV

But grief finds solace faint in others' ills
And but in her own shadow loves to go:
For her the mountain slide may crash and flow;
Alike to that dull eye the wild brook fills
With mist the chasm, or feeds the fields below;
Alike the latter rain with sure return
Breaks in the barren pine or thick distils
On the pond lily and the green brookflags
Or rises softly up to flood the fern.
What though the world were water drowned? or though
The sun, from his high place descending slow,
Should over the autumn landscapes brood and burn
Till all the vales were tinder, and their crags,
Apt to the touch of fire, Hephaestian hills?

∧ 3 *to* E and s *for*   *whose* E and s *the*
∨ 3: The diction of E and s is as follows:
   For her the mountain-side may flower or flow;

V

No shame dissuades his thought, no scorn despoils
Of beauty, who, the daily heaven beneath,
Gathers his bread by runsides, rocks and groves.
He drinks from rivers of a thousand soils,
And where broad Nature blows, he takes his breath:
For so his thought stands like the things he loves,
In thunderous purple like Cascadnac peak,
Or glimpses faint with grass and cinquefoils.
The friend may listen with a sneering cheek,
Concede the matter good and wish good luck,
Or plainly say, "Your brain is planet-struck!"
And drop your hoarded thought as vague and vain
Like bypast flowers, to redden again in rain,
Flung to the offal heap with shard and shuck.

No! cover not the fault. The wise revere
The judgment of the simple. Harshly flow
The words of counsel; but the end may show
Matter and music to the unwilling ear.
But perfect grief, like love, should cast out fear
And like an o'erbrimmed river moaning go.
Yet shrinks it from the senseless chaff and chat
Of those who smile and insolently bestow
Their ignorant praise, or those who stoop and peer
To pick with sharpened fingers for a flaw,
Nor ever touch the quick, nor rub the raw.
Better than this were surgery rough as that
Which, hammer and chisel in hand, at one sharp blow
Strikes out the wild tooth from a horse's jaw.

His heart was in his garden; but his brain
Wandered at will among the fiery stars.
Bards, heroes, prophets, Homers, Hamilcars,
With many angels stood, his eye to gain;
The devils, too, were his familiars:
And yet the cunning florist held his eyes
Close to the ground, a tulip bulb his prize,
And talked of tan and bonedust, cutworms, grubs,
As though all Nature held no higher strain;
Or, if he spoke of art, he made the theme
Flow through boxborders, turf, and flower tubs
Or, like a garden engine's, steered the stream,
Now spouted rainbows to the silent skies,
Now kept it flat and raked the walls and shrubs.

Companions were we in the grove and glen,
Through belts of summer wandered hour on hour,
Ransacking sward and swamp to deck his bower,
River and reservoir or mountain rain;
Nor sought for hard-named herb or plant of power,
But whippoorwill-shoe and quaint sidesaddle flower:
And still he talked, asserting thought is free
And wisest souls by their own action shine.
"For beauty," he said, "is seen where'er we look,
Growing alike in waste and guarded ground
And, like the May flower, gathered equally
On desolate hills, where scantily the pine
Drops his dry wisps about the barren rock,
And in the angles of the fences found."

But unto him came swift calamity
In the sweet springtime when his beds were green;
And my heart waited, trustfully serene,
For the new blossom on my household tree.
But flowers and gods and quaint philosophy
Are poor, in truth, to fill the empty place;
Nor any joy nor season's jollity
Can aught indeed avail to grace our grief.
Can spring return to him a brother's face,
Or bring my darling back to me—to me?
Undimmed the May went on with bird and bower;
The summer filled and faded like a flower;
But rainy autumn and the red-turned leaf
Found us at tears and wept for company.

X

Thy baby too, the child that was to be
Through happier days—a brightening sun above—
Held to thy heart with more forgetful love,
So proud a portion of thyself and me:
We talked it o'er,—the bliss that was to bless;
The birth, the baby robes, the christening,
And all our hearts were carried in this thing.
Cold, cold she lies where houseless tempests blow.
The baby's face is here, almost a woe;
And I, so seared in soul, so sapped and shrunk,
Gaze hopeless,—careless, in my changed estate
To fall at once, or in the wilderness
Stand like a charred and fire-hardened trunk,
To break the axe's edge of time and fate.

XI

Still pressing through these weeping solitudes,
Perchance I snatch a beam of comfort bright
And pause to fix the gleam or lose it quite
That darkens as I move or but intrudes
To baffle and forelay: as sometimes here,
When late at night the waried engineer
Driving his engine up through Whately woods
Sees on the track a glimmering lantern light
And checks his crashing speed, with hasty hand
Reversing and retarding;—but again,
Look where it burns, a furlong on before!
The witchlight of the reedy rivershore,
The pilot of the forest and the fen,
Not to be left, but with the waste woodland.

XII

How most unworthy, echoing in mine ears,
The verse sounds on: life, love, experience, art
Fused into grief and, like a grief-filled heart
Where all emotion tends and turns to tears,
Broken by its own strength of passion and need;
Unworthy, though the bitter waters start
In these dim eyes, reviewing thought and word:
The high desire, the faint accomplished deed,
Unuttered love and loss, and feverish
Beatings against a gate forever barred.
Yet over and again I range and read
The blotted page, returning leaf and leaf,
And half-believe the words are what I wish,
And pore upon my verse, and court my grief,—

XIII

Even as a lover, dreaming, unaware,
Calls o'er his mistress' features hour by hour,
Nor thinks of simple dress and humble dower
But pictures to himself her graces rare,—
Dark eyes, dark lashes, and harmonious hair
Caught lightly up with amaryllis flower,
Haemanthus, eardrop, or auricula,
And deems within wide Nature's bound and law
All to beseem her beauty but designed,
Of pure or proud, nor counts himself too bold
To fit her forehead with the perfect gold
Or round her girlish temples belt and bind
Some lamp of jewels, lovelier than the whole,
Green diamond, or gem of girasol!

XIV

The breeze is sharp, the sky is hard and blue,
Blue with white tails of cloud: on such a day,
Upon a neck of sand o'erblown with spray,
We stood in silence the great sea to view.
And mark the bathers at their shuddering play
Run in and out with the succeeding wave,
While from our footsteps broke the trembling turf:—
Again I hear the drenching of the wave;
The rocks rise dark, with wall and weedy cave;
Her voice is in mine ears, her answer yet:
Again I see above the froth and fret
The blue loft standing like eternity
And white feet flying from the surging surf
And simmering suds of the sea!

v 5 mark E and s marked   shuddering ORIG:shivering   9 dark E and
s dim

[25]

XV

Gertrude and Gulielma, sister-twins,
Dwelt in the valley at the farmhouse old;
Nor grief had touched their locks of dark and gold
Nor dimmed the fragrant whiteness of their skins:
Both beautiful, and one in height and mould;
Yet one had loveliness which the spirit wins
To other worlds: eyes, forehead, smile and all,
More softly serious than the twilight's fall.
The other—can I e'er forget the day
When, stealing from a laughing group away,
To muse with absent eye and motion slow,
Her beauty fell upon me like a blow?—
Gertrude! with red flowerlip, and silk black hair!
Yet Gulielma was by far more fair.

Under the mountain, as when first I knew
Its low dark roof and chimney creeper-twined,
The red house stands; and yet my footsteps find,
Vague in the walks, waste balm and feverfew.
But they are gone: no soft-eyed sisters trip
Across the porch or lintels; where, behind,
The mother sat, sat knitting with pursed lip.
The house stands vacant in its green recess,
Absent of beauty as a broken heart.
The wild rain enters, and the sunset wind
Sighs in the chambers of their loveliness
Or shakes the pane—and in the silent noons
The glass falls from the window, part by part,
And ringeth faintly in the grassy stones.

v 2 *dark* E and s *black*   14 *ringeth* MS *tinkles*

Roll on, sad world! not Mercury or Mars
Could swifter speed, or slower, round the sun
Than in this year of variance thou hast done
To me: yet pain, fear, heart-break, woes and wars
Have natural limit; from his dread eclipse
The swift sun hastens, and the night debars
The day but to bring in the day more bright.
The flowers renew their odorous fellowships;
The moon runs round and round, the slow earth dips,
True to her poise, and lifts; the planet-stars
Roll and return from circle to ellipse;
The day is dull and soft, the eavetrough drips,
And yet I know the splendor of the light
Will break anon. Look! where the gray is white!

XVIII

And change with hurried hand has swept these scenes:
The woods have fallen, across the meadow-lot
The hunter's trail and trap-path is forgot,
And fire has drunk the swamps of evergreens;
Yet for a moment let my fancy plant
These autumn hills again: the wild dove's haunt,
The wild deer's walk. In golden umbrage shut,
The Indian river runs, Quonecktacut!
Here, but a lifetime back, where falls tonight
Behind the curtained pane a sheltered light
On buds of rose or vase of violet
Aloft upon the marble mantel set,
Here in the forest-heart, hung blackening
The wolfbait on the bush beside the spring.

∧ 4 *To* E and s *For*

XIX

And faces, forms and phantoms, numbered not,
Gather and pass like mist upon the breeze,
Jading the eye with uncouth images:
Women with muskets, children dropping shot
By fields half harvested or left in fear
Of Indian inroad, or the Hessian near;
Disaster, poverty, and dire disease.
Or from the burning village, through the trees
I see the smoke in reddening volumes roll,
The Indian file in shadowy silence pass
While the last man sets up the trampled grass,
The Tory priest declaiming, fierce and fat,
The Shay's man with the green branch in his hat,
Or silent sagamore, Shaug or Wassahoale.

O hard endeavor, to blend in with these
Dark shadings of the past a darker grief
Or blur with stranger woes a wound so chief,
Though the great world turn slow with agonies.
What though the forest windflowers fell and died
And Gertrude sleeps at Gulielma's side?
They have their tears, nor turn to us their eyes:
But we pursue our dead with groans and cries
And bitter reclamations to the term
Of undiscerning darkness and the worm;
Then sit in silence down and darkly dwell
Through the slow years on all we loved, and tell
Each tone, each look of love, each syllable,
With lips that work, with eyes that overwell.

v 2 *Dark* E *Deep*   *darker* E *deeper*   11 *darkly* E and s *brooding*

[28]

Last night I dreamed we parted once again;
That all was over. From the outward shore
I saw a dim bark lessen more and more,
That bore her from me o'er the boundless main,
And yearned to follow: no sense of mystery
Fell on me nor the old fear of the sea.
Only I thought, knowledge must bring relief,
Nor feared the sunless gulfs, the tempest's breath,
Nor drowning, nor the bitterness of death.
Yet while as one who sees his hope decay,
And scarcely weeping, vacant in my grief,
I on the jetty stood and watched the ship,
The wave broke fresher, flinging on my lip
Some drops of salt. I shuddered, and turned away.

XXII

Put off thy bark from shore, though near the night,
And leaving home and friends and hope behind,
Sail down the lights. Thou scarce canst fail to find,
O desolate one, the morning breaking white,
Some shore of rest beyond the laboring wave.
Ah, 'tis for this I mourn: too long I have
Wandered in tears along life's stormy way
Where day to day no haven or hope reveals.
Yet on the bound my weary sight I keep
As one who sails, a landsman on the deep,
And longing for the land, day after day
Sees the horizon rise and fall and feels
His heart die out, still riding restlessly
Between the sailing cloud and the seasick sea.

∧ 3 *dim* E and MS *dark*

XXIII

Some truths indeed may pierce the spirit's gloom,
Yet shine unapprehended: grand, remote;
We bow before their strength, yet feel them not—
When some low promise of the life to come,
Blessing the mourner, holds the heart indeed,
A leading lamp that all may reach and read—
Nor reck those lights, so distant over us,
Sublime, yet helpless to the spirit's need
As the night stars in heaven's vault: yet thus
While the great asterisms mount and burn
Unheeded for their glory, this its height
Has reached, but lingers on till light return,
Low in the sky, like frosty Sirius,
To snap and sparkle through the winter's night.

XXIV

Each common object too, the house, the grove,
The street, the face, the ware in the window, seems
Alien and sad, the wreck of perished dreams;
Painfully present, yet remote in love.
The day goes down in rain, the winds blow wide.
I leave the town; I climb the mountain side,
Striving from stumps and stones to wring relief,
And in the senseless anger of my grief,
I rave and weep, I roar to the unmoved skies;
But the wild tempest carries away my cries.
Then back I turn to hide my face in sleep,
Again with dawn the same dull round to sweep,
And buy and sell and prate and laugh and chide,
As if she had not lived, or had not died.

ʌ 1 *Some truths indeed may pierce the spirit's* E and S *Some truths may
pierce the spirit's deeper* 8 *yet* E and S *but* 10 *While* E and S *Though*
11 *Unheeded for their* E and S *In inaccessible*

XXV

Small gossip, whispering at the window-pane,
Finds reason still for aught beneath the sun,
Answers itself ere answer shall be none
And in the personal field delights to reign—
Meting to this his grief, to that his gain,
And busy to detract, to head or hang.
O wiser far, for him who lieth hid
Within himself, secure like him to stay,
Icesius' son who, when the city rang,
Knew there was news abroad nor wondered what.
If these conspire, why should I counterplot
Or vex my heart with guessing whether or not
John went to church, or what my neighbor did
The day before day before yesterday?

XXVI

Yet from indifference may we hope for peace,
Or in inaction lose the sense of pain?
Joyless I stand, with vacant heart and brain,
And scarce would turn the hand to be or cease.
No onward purpose in my life seems plain:
Today may end it, or tomorrow will;
Life still to be preserved, though worthless still,
A tear-dimmed face, glassed in a gilded locket.
But conscience, starting with a reddening cheek,
Loud on the ear her homely message sends,
"Ere the sun plunge, determine, up! awake!
And for thy sordid being make amends;
Truth is not found by feeling in the pocket,
Nor wisdom sucked from out the fingers' ends!"

v 14 *ends* E and s *end*

XXVII

But the heart murmurs at so harsh a tone.
So sunk in tears it lies, so gone in grief,
With its own blood 'twould venture, far more lief,
Than underprize one drop of sorrow's own
Or grudge one hour of mournful idleness.
To idle time indeed—to moan our moan
And then go shivering from a folded gate,
Broken in heart and life, exheredate
Of all we loved: yet some, from dire distress,
Accounting tears no loss and grief no crime,
Have gleaned up gold and made their walk sublime.
So he, poor wanderer in steps like theirs,
May find *his* griefs, though it must be with tears,
Gold grit and grail, washed from the sands of time.

XXVIII

Yet sometimes, with the sad respectant mind
We look upon lost hours of want and wail
As on a picture, with contentment pale;
And even the present seems with voices kind
To soothe our sorrow; and the past endears;
Or like a sick man's happy trance appears,
When on the first soft waves of slumber's calm
And like a wreck that has outlived the gale,
No longer lifted by the wrenching billow,
He rides at rest; while from the distant dam,
Dim and far off as in a dream, he hears
The pulsing hammer play, or the vague wind
Rising and falling in the wayside willow,
Or the faint rustling of the watch beneath his pillow.

∧ 13: *his*. The word is italicized in MS and E.

XXIX

How oft in schoolboy-days, from the school's sway
Have I run forth to Nature as to a friend,
With some pretext of o'erwrought sight, to spend
My schooltime in green meadows far away!
Careless of summoning bell or clocks that strike,
I marked with flowers the minutes of my day.
For still the eye that shrank from hated hours,
Dazzled with decimal and dividend,
Knew each bleached alder root that plashed across
The bubbling brook, and every mass of moss;
Could tell the month, too, by the vervain-spike,
How far the ring of purple tiny flowers
Had climbed—just starting, maybe, with the May,
Half-high, or tapering off at summer's end.

XXX

Yet even mid merry boyhood's tricks and scapes,
Early my heart a deeper lesson learnt:
Wandering alone by many a mile of burnt
Black woodside, that but the snowflake decks and drapes;
And I have stood beneath Canadian sky
In utter solitudes, where the cricket's cry
Appals the heart, and fear takes visible shapes;
And on Long Island's void and isolate capes
Heard the sea break like iron bars. And still
In all I seemed to hear the same deep dirge
Borne in the wind, the insect's tiny trill,
And crash and jangle of the shaking surge,
And knew not what they meant, prophetic woe?
Dim bodings wherefore? Now indeed I know.

XXXI

My Anna! when for thee my head was bowed,
The circle of the world, sky, mountain, main,
Drew inward to one spot: and now again
Wide Nature narrows to the shell and shroud.
In the late dawn they will not be forgot,
And evenings early-dark, when the low rain
Begins at nightfall, though no tempests rave,
I know the rain is falling on her grave.
The morning views it, and the sunset cloud
Points with a finger to that lonely spot:
The crops that up the valley rolling go
Ever towards her slumber bow and blow.
I look on the sweeping corn and the surging rye,
And with every gust of wind my heart goes by.

XXXII

O for the face and footstep! woods and shores
That looked upon us in life's happiest flush,
That saw our figures breaking from the brush;
That heard our voices calling through the bowers,
How are ye darkened! Deepest tears upgush
From the heart's heart, gathering more and more
Blindness and strangling tears, as now before
Your shades I stand and find ye still so fair.
And thou, sad mountain stream, thy stretches steal
Through fern and flag as when we gathered flowers
Along thy reeds and shallows cold, or where—
Over the red reef with a rolling roar—
The woods through glimmering gaps of green reveal,
Sideward, the river turning like a wheel.

ʌ 1 *thee* s *her*

ᵥ 6 *heart, gathering* MS *heart: & gathering*   14 *river* MS *River*

[34]

One still dark night I sat alone and wrote:
So still it was that distant Chanticleer
Seemed to cry out his warning at my ear,
Save for the brooding echo in his throat.
Sullen I sat, when like the nightwind's note
A voice said, "Wherefore doth he weep and fear?
Doth he not know no cry to God is dumb?"
Another spoke: "His heart is dimmed and drowned
With grief." I knew the shape that bended then
To kiss me, when suddenly I once again
Across the watches of the starless gloom
Heard the cock scream and pause: the morning bell
Into the gulfs of night dropped One! The vision fell
And left me listening to the sinking sound.

XXXIV

My Anna, though thine earthly steps are done,
Nor in the garden nor beside the door
Shall I behold thee standing any more,
I would not hide my face from light, nor shun
The full completion of this worldly day.
What though beside my feet no other one
May set her own to walk the forward way,
I will not fear to take the path alone,
Loving for thy sake things that cheer and bless,
Kind words, pure deeds, and gentlest charities.
Nor will I cease to hold a hope and aim
But, prophet-like, of these will make my bread
And feed my soul at peace, as Esdras fed
On flowers, until the vision and the glory came.

Nor all of solemn is my thought of her.
Though changed and glorified, must there not be
Place still for mirth and innocent gayety
And pure young hearts? Or do we gravely err,
And is their happiness too deep for joy?
It cannot be. The natural heart's employ
Pours praise as pure as any worshipper
Lost in his rite, too raptured to be gay.
Yes, and such service in its flight outstrips
The cries of suffering hearts that wail and bleed,
The groans of grief, crushed from some bitter need.
This is the faith I bear; and look indeed
To hear her laugh again and feel her lips
Kiss from my brow the heavy thoughts away.

Farewell, farewell, O noble heart! I dreamed
That time nor death could from my side divorce
Thy fair young life, beside whose pure bright course
My earthly nature stationary seemed:
Yet, by companionship, direction took
And progress, as the bank runs with the brook;
O round that mould which all thy mortal hath,
Our children's, and about my own sere path,
May these dim thoughts not fall as dry and vain
But fruitful as March dust or April rain,
Forerun the green, foretell the perfect day
Of restoration, when in fields divine,
And walking as of old, thy hand in mine,
By the still waters we may softly stray.

∧ 11 *crushed* E, S, and ORIG:*wrung*

∨ 4 *earthly* MS *earthy*

As Eponina brought, to move the king
In the old day, her children of the tomb,
Begotten and brought forth in charnel gloom
To plead a father's cause, so I too bring
Unto thy feet, my Maker, tearfully,
These offspring of my sorrow, hidden long
And scarcely able to abide the light.
May their deep cry, inaudible, come to Thee
Clear through the cloud of words, the sobs of song,
And sharper than that other's pierce thine ears:
That so each thought, aim, utterance, dark or bright,
May find thy pardoning love more blest than she
Who joyful passed with them to death and night,
With whom she had been buried nine long years.

This sonnet is unnumbered in MS.   4 *father's* MS *Father's*   8 *Thee*
s *thee*

SONNETS

Third Series, 1860-1872

*

I

Once on a day, alone but not elate,
I sat perusing a forgotten sage
And turning hopelessly a dim old page
Of history, long disused and out of date,
Reading "his Method" till I lost my own.
When suddenly there fell a gold presage
Of sunset sunshine on the letters thrown.
The day had been one cloud, but now a bird
Shot into song. I left my hermitage
With happy heart; but ere I reached the gate
The sun was gone, the bird, and bleak and drear,
All but an icy breath the balsams stirred:
I turned again and, entering with a groan,
Sat darkly down to Dagoraus Whear.

II

But Nature in her mood pushes or pulls
At her caprice; we see what is not shown
By that which we behold, nor this alone;
To commonest matters let us fix a bound
Or purport, straight another use is found
And this annihilates and that annuls.
And every straw of grass, or dirt, or stone,
Has different function from the kind well-known:
Commerce and custom, dikes and watermills.
Not to the sea alone, from inland earth,
The stream draws down its freight of floats and hulls,
But backward far, upwinding to the north,
The river gleams, a highway for the gulls
That fly not over land, into the hills.

∧ 12 *All but an* s *An all but*
∨ 8 *Has* ms *Have*

[41]

Yet not for him lifts the low weather cloud,
Not for his solace comes the clearing gale,
Who dreams but on himself, whose breath may fail
And leave no crown his due, no god his debtor;
Of his own gloom sole builder and begetter.
But Nature for thy mirth shall laugh aloud,
O trustful child, who on her heart hast lain
In every flow of storm and fit of rain.
So let the day be wilder, windier, wetter,
It irks not thee, nor bids thy fealty end,
Affection wasted and allegiance vain;
But rather seems like an embracing Friend
Who puts thee from him, but to view thee better,
And better so to fold thee close again.

IV

Thin little leaves of wood fern, ribbed and toothed,
Long curved sail needles of the green pitch pine,
With common sandgrass, skirt the horizon line,
And over these the incorruptible blue!
Here let me gently lie and softly view
All world asperities, lightly touched and smoothed
As by his gracious hand, the great Bestower.
What though the year be late? some colors run
Yet through the dry, some links of melody.
Still let me be, by such, assuaged and soothed
And happier made, as when, our schoolday done,
We hunted on from flower to frosty flower,
Tattered and dim, the last red butterfly,
Or the old grasshopper molasses-mouthed.

v 2: *curved sail needles*. Golden correctly notes that Bynner's "hyphenat-
ing of 'curv'd sail' produces a variation in the scene Tuckerman is describing. Tuckerman depicts the pine needles as curved like the needles used to
sew sails, while Bynner by his hyphenation alters the picture, giving the
reader an impression of pine needles curved like sails in a wind." (G, 43)
3 *With* s *And*

V

How well do I recall that walk in state
Across the Common, by the paths we knew:
Myself in silver badge and riband blue,
My little sister with her book and slate;
The elm tree by the Pond, the fence of wood,
The burial place that at the corner stood
Where once we crossed, through the forbidden grate,
The stones that grudg'd us way, the graveside weed,
The ominous wind that turned us half about.
Smit by the flying drops, at what a speed
Across the paths, unblessed and unforgiven
We hurried homeward when the day was late
And heard, with awe that left no place for doubt,
God's anger mutter in the darkened heaven.

VI

I looked across the rollers of the deep,
Long land-swells, ropes of weed, and riding foam,
With bitter angry heart: did I not roam
Ever like these? And what availeth sleep?
Or wakefulness? or pain? And still the sea
Rustled and sang, "Alike! and one to me!"
Ay! once I trod these shores too happily,
Murmuring my gladness to the rocks and ground
And, while the wave broke loud on ledge and reef,
Whispered it in the pause, like one who tells
His heart's dream and delight! And still the sea
Went back and forth upon its bar of shells,
Washed and withdrew, with a soft shaling sound,
As though the wet were dry and joy were grief.

∧ 7 *grate* s *gate*

[43]

O rest divine! O golden certainty
Of love! when love's half smile, illumining pain,
Bade all bright things immutable remain.
Dreaming I stand, the low brook drawling by,
Her flowerlike mien, her mountain step to mark.
Ah, I recall when her least look again
Could mar the music in my happy mind
And plunge me into doubt, her faintest sigh
Stir all the fixed pillars of my heaven,
Commingling them in mist and stormy dark!
And all together, as I have seen the rain
When the whole shower is swinging in the wind,
And like a mighty pendulum urged and driven,
Beat back and forth between the earth and sky!

As one turned round on some high mountain top
Views all things as they are, but out of place,
Reversing recognition, so I trace
Dimly those dreams of youth and love and stop
Blindly; for in such mood landmarks and ways
That we have trodden all our lives and know
We seem not to have known and cannot guess:
Like one who told his footsteps over to me
In the opposite world and where he wandered through
Whilst the hot wind blew from the sultry north—
Forests that give no shade, and bottomless
Sands where the plummet sinks as in the sea,
Saw the sky struck by lightning from the earth,
Rain salt like blood, and flights of fiery snow.

∧ 6 *Ah* s *Oh*

But into order falls our life at last,
Though in the retrospection jarred and blent.
Broken ambition, love misplaced or spent
Too soon, and slander busy with the past:
Sorrows too sweet to lose, or vexing joy.
But Time will bring oblivion of annoy,
And Silence bind the blows that words have lent;
And we will dwell, unheeding Love or Fame
Like him who has outlived a shining Name:
And Peace will come, as evening comes to him,
No leader now of men, no longer proud
But poor and private, watching the sun's rim;
Contented too, to fade as yonder cloud
Dim fades, and as the sun fades, fades alike, like dim.

x

Sometimes I walk where the deep water dips
Against the land. Or on where fancy drives
I walk and muse aloud, like one who strives
To tell his half-shaped thought with stumbling lips,
And view the ocean sea, the ocean ships,
With joyless heart: still but myself I find
And restless phantoms of my restless mind:
Only the moaning of my wandering words,
Only the wailing of the wheeling plover,
And this high rock beneath whose base the sea
Has wormed long caverns, like my tears in me:
And hard like this I stand, and beaten and blind,
This desolate rock with lichens rusted over,
Hoar with salt-sleet and chalkings of the birds.

ʌ 14 *fades alike, like dim* s *fading likewise dim*

Long Island! yes! When first my vision swept
Thy far faint shores with inlet and lagoon
Or misty woodflats, where the senses swoon
As in that land where Christian sank and slept,
I thought of him; and then when in the rain
We reached the Inn; but when I heard them speak
Of Fire Place at hand, and Devil's Neck,
And Good Ground and Mount Sinai west away,
As in a dream I seemed to tread again
The Pilgrim's steps and trace the Heavenly Way!
But there sat Happy Jack, with dumb Rejoice,
Red Ike the hostler with his whistling voice,
And an old man I called Legality . . .
Craftily quaint the tale he told to me.

XII

"Young Silas Long, a carrier through these woods,
Drove home one night in not the best of moods,
Having just seen a drowned man flung ashore
With a strange feather cap. And once before,
When he was hauling seine in Southold Bay
About this time of year, a seaman's corse
Washed up, with such a cap and such a face,
And it had brought misfortune on the place.
Pondering he drove; when lo, across the way
He saw, too late, that there a body lay,
Felt the wheels tilt but could not stop his horse
Or not at once, then—flinging with a slap
The old cloth cover down he called a cap—
Ran back, ten steps or more, and nothing found . . .

∧ 6 but s and

XIII

"Yes! the dead pines and deersfoot on the ground,—
So quick returned again in five or six:
His cap was gone and in its stead thrown down
The very loon-skin the twice-drowned had on,
With bits of seaweed sticking to the flix.
So Long rode home, of cap and sense bereft,
But still can show the dead man's that was left,
And the webs crawl, he says, when the sea rolls."
Then he, having told his tale and said his say,
By way of emphasis, or corollary,
Spat a torpedo in the bed of coals.
"And what, what, what," squealed Ike, "became of
        Long's?"
But the old man here rose and reached the tongs,
Laid fire to his pipe and phewed away.

XIV

An episode: yet with a relish rank
Of wild sea places—or of life indeed—
Where yet we find unstirred the secret seed
Of song or story marvellous, and thank
The sailor for his jest and manners rude.
More welcome, too, the old-fashioned fireside,
The beach of devils' aprons at low tide,
Than scandal bleeding-new, or journal dank.
Here did my dreaming childhood, listening, brood
On tales of wind and shipwreck; journeyings made
Island or inland; peaks at sea descried
Shaped like a wave, a table, or a tooth:
Old Peter Batte, that should be Pitherbooth,
Gibraltar's, or the grim Rock of Visgrade.

But we are set to strive to make our mark
And scarcely pause to plead for any play
Nor think that any hour of any day
Writes its own record down in chalk or chark,
For all we falsely claim or blindly say,
"I am the Truth, the Life too and the Way."
It stands, a word to comfort and appal,
A summons grave and sweet, a warning stark.
But death and dread responsibility
I hardly fear tonight, or feel at all:
Watching my fancy gleam, now bright, now dark,
As snapping from the brands a single spark
Splits in a spray of sparkles ere it fall,
And the long flurrying flame that shoots to die . . .

5 *or* s *and*

SONNETS

Fourth Series, 1860-1872

*

Still, like a city, seated on a height
Appears my soul, and gathered in her place:
Whilst, faintly hovering, swarm about her base,
Still nearer drawing with the nearer night,
Dim cloudlike groups of men and groups of horse,
Outposts and riders of some mightier Force
That lies along the hills; while from them thrown
Rise shadowing shafts with storms of summoning stone,
And the bolt falleth where the cross-bolt fell;
Till Doubt contends with Hope, and Fear conspires
To thwart them both: so that the soul retires
Even to her inmost keep and citadel
And views along the horizon darkening far,
Vague tumult, lights of woe, and moving war.

II

But Thought, like a mailed archer helmed and tall,
Treads ever on the outward battlement,
Striving to pierce—through embrasure and rent—
The secret of the gloom that girdleth all,
The immeasurable gulf and interval,
Nor heeds the random showers about him sent—
But whilst the cloudy squadrons tramp and wheel,
Busy with weight and bar and implement,
He casteth where to make his missiles fall—
Training his engine now, now lower, now higher,
As a strong archer sets his bow of steel.
Yet some may pass like meteors to the mark
Of those blind ventures loosed into the dark:
So swift the arrow flies, it taketh fire.

And thus the mind by its own impulse deep,
As lightning instantly enlighteneth,
May cleave the shades of sin, the shapes of death
That pace it round all day and never sleep,
That watch the wall all night and pace it round—
Yet not its own. In man's extremity
God lends the light we use, the strength we keep.
So let us use that light, that we may be
Oh, not perhaps with others thronged and crowned
But at the last in white arrayment found,—
So daily use it, that the mystery
Of life we touch: in cloud and wind and tree,
In human faces that about us dwell,
And the deep soul that knoweth heaven and hell.

IV

Yes, pray thy God to give, whate'er thou art,
Some work to be by thee with reverence wrought:
Some trumpet note obeyed, some good fight fought,
Ere thou lay down thy weapons and depart.
Brood on thyself, until thy lamp be spent;
Bind all thy force to compass and invent;
But shun the reveries of voluptuous thought,
Day-musings, the floralia of the heart
And vain imaginations: else may start
Beside the portals of thy tower or tent,
Rending thy trance with dissonant clang and jar,
A summons that shall drive thee wild to hear—
Loud, as when in the dreaming conqueror's ear
Antigenidas blew a point of war.

λ 12 *we touch* s *be touched*

v 10 *Beside* MS *Besides   portals* s *portal*

V

Yet some there be, believers for the nonce,
Who God's commands unwelcomely obey.
Lost in the path, they keep the heavenward way
But trip at absolute heaven and drop at once
In the red gulf: not so do thou essay
To snatch the splendor and to see the thrones.
Take patience, hope, nor miserably mourn;
If evil sneereth, yet abides the good.
Even now, could we look where the white ones wait
Nigh before God, and for a moment scan
The angelic faces; even though we stood
In audience of their voices, could we learn
More than 'tis love that lifts us near their state,
And the dear fellow aid of man to man.

VI

And two I knew, an old man and a boy,
Alternate helpers: for their day was spent
In gathering forest bark; and when they went
Late home, the elder did his time employ
To teach the other and tell him what he knew
Of history, myth, or mathematics hard,
In hours of night and, when the night was dark,
Showed him Job's Coffin, and the Golden Yard,
Showed the nine moonstars in the moonless blue,
And the great Circle of the Bestiary;
So that the child grew up to love the sky
And, in the woods beyond the hemlock bark,
To heed the intricate moss that o'er it grew,
The shadowy flower all wet with all-day dew.

 ∧ 8: *If evil sneereth.* I follow Bynner, who here resolved what seems to
have been a doubt in Tuckerman's mind. ms reads
　　　　　　　　If ill∧ sneereth, yet abides the good.
　9 *Even now,* s *And even*　The final sentence of the poem in ms is condi-
tional and declarative. Bynner made of it a question.

But war his overturning trumpet blew.
And in that scattering blast, the knot was rent
That held them: one his faint steps northward bent,
The younger the blind lot of battle drew;
And all seemed well, no cause for tears or joy;
But tidings came, or else, of these in lieu,
A written word: a hand, though rough to see,
The old man loved, for he had taught the boy.
At length all ceased: the last one *was* the last;
But still he read and with a fond belief
Weighed each, as 'twere to find some link or clue.
It never came,—but days the old man passed
Pondering upon the letters wistfully,
Silent, and with the fiery eye of grief.

Nor strange it is, to us who walk in bonds
Of flesh and time, if virtue's self awhile
Gleam dull like sunless ice; whilst graceful guile—
Blood-flecked like hamatite or diamonds
With a red inward spark—to reconcile
Beauty and evil seems and corresponds
So well with good that the mind joys to have
Full wider jet and scope: nor swings and sleeps
Forever in one cradle wearily
Like those vast weeds that off d'Acunha's isle
Wash with the surf and flap their mighty fronds
Mournfully to the dipping of the wave,
Yet cannot be disrupted from their deeps
By the whole heave and settle of the sea.

Here, where the red man swept the leaves away
To dig for cordial bark or cooling root,
The wayside apple drops its surly fruit.
Right through the deep heart of his midmost wood,
Through range and river and swampy solitude,
The common highway landward runs today,
The train booms by with long derisive hoot
And, following fast, rise factory, school, and forge.
I heed them not; but where yon alders shoot,
Searching strange plants to medicine my mood—
With a quick savage sense I stop, or stray
Through the brush pines and up the mountain gorge:
With patient eye, and with as safe a foot,
As though I walked the wood with sagamore George.

X

Hast thou seen reversed the prophet's miracle—
The worm that, touched, a twig-like semblance takes?
Or hast thou mused what giveth the craft that makes
The twirling spider at once invisible,
And the spermal odor to the barberry flower,
Or heard the singing sand by the cold coast foam,
Or late—in inland autumn groves afar—
Hast thou ever plucked the little chick-wintergreen star
And tasted the sour of its leaf? Then come
With me betimes, and I will show thee more
Than these, of nature's secrecies the least:
In the first morning, overcast and chill,
And in the day's young sunshine, seeking still
For earliest flowers and gathering to the east.

SONNETS

Fifth Series, 1860-1872

*

I

But Nature where she gives must give in kind,
Grant to the rich and from the poor withhold;
And much that we in manifest behold
Is faint to some, while other some still find
Truths—that to our sense may be veiled and furled—
Published as light, notorious as wind.
But the old Mother moves about her fire.
Replenishes its flame and feeds the world
And so fulfils her births and offices—
Causal or consequential cares not she
Or ortive or abortive: her desire
Is but to serve, and her necessity.
The invention and authority are His,
In the whole past or what remains to be.

II

Nor, though she seem to cast with backward hand
Strange measure, sunny cold or cloudy heat,
Or break with stamping rain the farmer's wheat,
Yet in such waste no waste the soul descries,
Intent to glean by barrenest sea and land.
For whoso waiteth, long and patiently,
Will see a movement stirring at his feet—
If he but wait nor think himself much wise.
Nay, from the mind itself a glimpse will rest
Upon the dark; summoning from vacancy
Dim shapes about his intellectual lamp,
Calling these in and causing him to see;
As the night-heron waking in the swamp
Lights up the pools with her phosphoric breast.

∧ 5 *may be* s *are*
∨ 9 *from* s *for*

[59]

And yet tonight, when summer daylight dies,
I crossed the fields against the summer gust
And with me, rising from my feet like dust,
A crowd of flea-like grasshoppers, like flies
Presaging dry and dry continuance; yet
Where they prefigure change, all signals must
Fail in the dry when they forebode the wet . . .
I know not. All tonight seemed mystery:
From the full fields that pressed so heavily,
The burden of the blade, the waste of blowth,
The twinkling of the smallest life that flits
To where, and all unconsciously, he sits:
My little boy, symbolling eternity,
Like the god Brahma, with his toe in his mouth.

IV

But man finds means, grant him but place and room,
To gauge the depths and views a wonder dawn,
Sees all the worlds in utmost space withdrawn
In shape and structure like a honeycomb,
Locates his sun and grasps the universe
Or to their bearings bids the orbs disperse;
Now seems to stand like that great angel girt
With moon and stars: now, sick for shelter even,
Craves but a roof to turn the thunder-rain—
Or finds his vaunted reach and wisdom vain,
Lost in the myriad meaning of a word,
Or starts at its bare import, panic-stirred:
For earth is earth or hearth or dearth or dirt,
The sky heaved over our faint heads is heaven.

V

Where will the ladder land? Who knows?—who knows?
He who would seize the planet zone by zone
As on a battlemarch, for use alone,
Nor stops for visionary wants and woes
But like the Bruce's, on, his heart he throws
And leaves behind the dreamer and the drone?
Great is his work indeed, his service great,
Who seeks for Nature but to subjugate,
Break and bereave, build upward and create
And, hampering her, to carry heave and drag
Points to results,—towns, cables, cars and ships.
Whilst I in dim green meadows lean and lag,
He counts his course in truth by vigorous steps,
By steps of stairs; but I add crag to crag.

VI

Licentiate of the schools, with knowledge hot,
A stranger hither came—our dames to frighten—
Who talked to us of Christ, the Sybil's grot,
Glanced at Copernick, though he knew him not,
And showed us hell and where the blest abide.
"The stars," he said, "that round the North-star glide—
For *there* is heaven—tell nightly as they brighten."
"But do they move?" I said. "Or is it so?"
He answered tranquilly, "We see they do."
It was enough. The crowd was satisfied,
And I was hushed—yet felt my color heighten.
Was he a knave, a coxcomb, or a clown,
Who stooping thus, our ignorance to enlighten,
Ended by so illuminating his own?

That night the town turned out and crammed the hall.
And I, perhaps maliciously, made one
To hear the lecture: I, who went to none,
And an old friend with me, who went to all.
But vain it were that thesis to recall,
A rant of phrase and metaphor blundered through
And meaning not or how, when ended quite
And poetry had closed what prayer begun,
Strong men were touched to tears and bright lips grew
Breathless with praise. But my companion
Spoke not, or spoke with satire grave and arch:
"We scarce had had such learning and such light
Since he, the Yankee schoolmaster, last March
Came from Nine Partners to Illyria down."

A garden lodge, shut in with quaintest growth,
A slender girl with still kine pasturing near,
And bright look half-expectant—need I fear
Thus to recall that morning when we both
Rode on to the wide city, loud and drear?
Yes, in the shock and tumult hurrying here,
Let me remind thee of that place of peace:
The maiden's smile, the look of happy doubt.
Nor in the stream of things, do thou too fail
Still to remember me of more than these:—
The little valley hidden in the pine,
The low-built cottage buried in the vale,
Wooded and over-wooded, bushed about
With holm tree, ople tree, and sycamine.

For these, my friend, were but the foldings fair,
The furling leaves about the jewel-flower,
The shade that lent her beauty half its dower,—
The beauty that made rich the shadow there,
Touching all objects with transfiguring power:
The housedog at the door, the village school,
The village in the hills, the hills of Ule . . .
And thou, Aurania, with thy brow of pearl,
So loved from all the world, didst overrule
All time, all thought, in thy sweet kingdom, girl!
Through the slow weeks my fancy found but her
And day by day at dusk and dawn-break cool:
All the long moonlight nights I dreamed of Ule
And in the dark half of the months my heart was there.

X

A poet's moonshine! Yes, for love must lend
Answer to reason, though 'tis bitter breath.
Better wild roses died their natural death
Than evilly or idly them to rend.
The girl was fair as flower the moon beneath,
Gentle and good, and constant to her friend,
Yet out of her own place, not so complete:
Was wedded to her kind—had leave to lack,
But old associations rarely slip.
Tight as a stem of grass within its sheath,
You yet may draw and nibble, touch the sweet
With the tip tongue and browse the tender end
Half-vacantly; but not to be put back,
Or swallowed in, but sputtered from the lip.

XI

Another: opposite as sky and lands—
As distant too, thy beauty gleams on me.
Bend downward from thy heaven of chastity
And I will reach with earthy flickering hands.
For I am grim and stained, thou white and shrined.
'Tis better so. No common love our doom,
Half-nursed, half-forced, in common cold and gloom—
But quick, convulsively, our souls shall strike
And, in the dance of life, tumultuous wind
Like fresh and salt indeed. O thus may we
Join instantly, like to the cloud and sea
In whirling pillar!—nor meet in darkness like
Stalactite and stalagmite, ignorantly
Nearing each other, slow and of one kind.

'Twas granted:—but the bitter god of Love,
As in revenge for some disparagement,
Left us to strive, inextricably blent,
Before we knew in truth for what we strove,
Or why we went, unwillingly, who went,
Or whether driven, or who he was that drove.
The countless haps that draw vague heart to heart,
The countless hands that push true hearts apart—
Of these we nothing recked, and nothing knew.
The wonder of the world, the faint surmise,
The clouded looks of hate, the harrowing eyes,
But pierced and pinned together: 'twas one to us.
With the same arrow smitten through and through,
We fell, like Phadimus and Tantalus.

A wash of rippling breath that just arrives,
Thin yellow tufts shattering and showering down
And, underfoot and all about me blown,
Thin yellow tufts and threads, bunches of fives:
Too curiously I note each lightest thing.
But where are they, my friends whose fair young lives
Gave these dead bowers the freshness of the spring?
Gone! And save tears and memory, all is gone . . .
Fate robs us not of these nor Death deprives.
But when will Nature here new beauty bring
Or thou behold those faces gathering?
I mark the glimmering moss that yet survives,
I touch the trees, I tread the shedded shives,—
But when will come the new awakening?

And me my winter's task is drawing over,
Though night and winter shake the drifted door.
Critic or friend, dispraiser or approver,
I come not now nor fain would offer more.
But when buds break and round the fallen limb
The wild weeds crowd in clusters and corymb,
When twilight rings with the red robin's plaint,
Let me give something—though my heart be faint—
To thee, my more than friend!—believer! lover!
The gust has fallen now, and all is mute—
Save pricking on the pane the sleety showers,
The clock that ticks like a belated foot,
Time's hurrying step, the twanging of the hours:
Wait for those days, my friend, or get thee fresher flowers.

Let me give something!—though my spring be done,
Give to the children, ere their summertime:
Though stirred with grief, like rain let fall my rhyme
And tell of one whose aim was much, of one
Whose strife was this: that in his thought should be
Some power of wind, some drenching of the sea,
Some drift of stars across a darkling coast,
Imagination, insight, memory, awe,
And dear New England nature first and last,—
Whose end was high, whose work was well-begun:
Of one who from his window looked and saw
His little hemlocks in the morning sun,
And while he gazed, into his heart almost
The peace that passeth understanding passed.

XVI

Let me give something!—as the years unfold,
Some faint fruition, though not much, my most:
Perhaps a monument of labor lost.
But thou, who givest all things, give not me
To sink in silence, seared with early cold,
Frost-burnt and blackened, but quick fire for frost!
As once I saw at a houseside, a tree
Struck scarlet by the lightning, utterly
To its last limb and twig: so strange it seemed,
I stopped to think if this indeed were May,
And were those windflowers? or had I dreamed?
But there it stood, close by the cottage eaves,
Red-ripened to the heart: shedding its leaves
And autumn sadness on the dim spring day.

THE CRICKET

*

THE CRICKET

I

The humming bee purrs softly o'er his flower;
   From lawn and thicket
The dogday locust singeth in the sun
   From hour to hour:
Each has his bard, and thou, ere day be done,   5
   Shalt have no wrong.
So bright that murmur mid the insect crowd,
Muffled and lost in bottom-grass, or loud
   By pale and picket:
Shall I not take to help me in my song   10
   A little cooing cricket?

II

The afternoon is sleepy; let us lie
Beneath these branches whilst the burdened brook,
Muttering and moaning to himself, goes by;
And mark our minstrel's carol whilst we look   15
Toward the faint horizon swooning blue.
   Or in a garden bower,
Trellised and trammeled with deep drapery
   Of hanging green,
   Light glimmering through—   20
There let the dull hop be,
Let bloom, with poppy's dark refreshing flower:
Let the dead fragrance round our temples beat,
Stunning the sense to slumber, whilst between
The falling water and fluttering wind   25
   Mingle and meet,
   Murmur and mix,

No few faint pipings from the glades behind,
  Or alder-thicks:
But louder as the day declines,   30
From tingling tassel, blade, and sheath,
Rising from nets of river vines,
  Winrows and ricks,
  Above, beneath,
  At every breath,   35
At hand, around, illimitably
Rising and falling like the sea,
  Acres of cricks!

III

Dear to the child who hears thy rustling voice
Cease at his footstep, though he hears thee still,   40
Cease and resume with vibrance crisp and shrill,
Thou sittest in the sunshine to rejoice.
Night lover too; bringer of all things dark
And rest and silence; yet thou bringest to me
Always that burthen of the unresting Sea,   45
The moaning cliffs, the low rocks blackly stark;
These upland inland fields no more I view,
But the long flat seaside beach, the wild seamew,
  And the overturning wave!
Thou bringest too, dim accents from the grave   50
To him who walketh when the day is dim,
Dreaming of those who dream no more of him,
With edged remembrances of joy and pain;
And heyday looks and laughter come again:
Forms that in happy sunshine lie and leap,   55
With faces where but now a gap must be,
Renunciations, and partitions deep
And perfect tears, and crowning vacancy!
And to thy poet at the twilight's hush,
No chirping touch of lips with laugh and blush,   60
But wringing arms, hearts wild with love and woe,
Closed eyes, and kisses that would not let go!

So wert thou loved in that old graceful time
   When Greece was fair,
While god and hero hearkened to thy chime;   65
   Softly astir
Where the long grasses fringed Caÿster's lip;
Long-drawn, with glimmering sails of swan and ship,
   And ship and swan;
     Or where   70
   Reedy Eurotas ran.
Did that low warble teach thy tender flute
   Xenaphyle?
Its breathings mild? say! did the grasshopper
Sit golden in thy purple hair   75
   O Psammathe?
     Or wert thou mute,
Grieving for Pan amid the alders there?
And by the water and along the hill
That thirsty tinkle in the herbage still,   80
Though the lost forest wailed to horns of Arcady?

V

Like the Enchanter old—
Who sought mid the dead water's weeds and scum
For evil growths beneath the moonbeam cold,
   Or mandrake or dorcynium;   85
And touched the leaf that opened both his ears,
So that articulate voices now he hears
In cry of beast, or bird, or insect's hum,—
Might I but find thy knowledge in thy song!
   That twittering tongue,   90
Ancient as light, returning like the years.
   So might I be,
Unwise to sing, thy true interpreter

76: *Psammathe.* Probably Psamathe, the mother of Linos.

Through denser stillness and in sounder dark,
Than ere thy notes have pierced to harrow me.   95
  So might I stir
  The world to hark
  To thee my lord and lawgiver,
  And cease my quest:
Content to bring thy wisdom to the world;   100
Content to gain at last some low applause,
  Now low, now lost
Like thine from mossy stone, amid the stems and straws,
  Or garden gravemound tricked and dressed—
  Powdered and pearled   105
  By stealing frost—
In dusky rainbow beauty of euphorbias!
For larger would be less indeed, and like
The ceaseless simmer in the summer grass
To him who toileth in the windy field,   110
  Or where the sunbeams strike,
Naught in innumerable numerousness.
  So might I much possess,
  So much must yield;
But failing this, the dell and grassy dike,   115
The water and the waste shall still be dear,
And all the pleasant plots and places
  Where thou hast sung, and I have hung
  To ignorantly hear.
Then Cricket, sing thy song! or answer mine!   120
Thine whispers blame, but mine has naught but praises.
It matters not. Behold! the autumn goes,
  The shadow grows,
The moments take hold of eternity;
Even while we stop to wrangle or repine   125
  Our lives are gone—
  Like thinnest mist,
Like yon escaping color in the tree;
Rejoice! rejoice! whilst yet the hours exist—
Rejoice or mourn, and let the world swing on   130
Unmoved by cricket song of thee or me.

THE PUBLISHED POEMS

*

The published poems appear here in the order in which they are contained in manuscript and in the *Poems* of 1860, 1863, 1864, and 1869. *November* is one of the five sonnets not contained in s. The remaining four are: "April"; "Again, again ye part in stormy grief"; and the sonnet sequence, "The starry flower, the flowerlike stars that fade." s contains 106 sonnets; therefore, Golden's statement that Tuckerman wrote a total of 109 sonnets is incorrect. (G, 42)

November

Oh! who is there of us that has not felt
The sad decadence of the failing year,
And marked the lesson still with grief and fear
Writ in the rolled leaf and widely dealt?
When now no longer burns yon woodland belt
Bright with disease; no tree in glowing death
Leans forth a cheek of flame to fade and melt
In the warm current of the west wind's breath;
Nor yet through low blue mist on slope and plain
Droops the red sunlight in a dream of day;
But from that lull the winds of change have burst
And dashed the drowsy leaf with shattering rain,
And swung the groves, and roared, and wreaked their worst
Till all the world is harsh and cold and gray.

April

The first of April! yet November's haze
Hangs on the wood, and blurs the hill's blue tip:
The light of noon rests wanly on the strip
Of sandy road, recalling leaf-laid ways,
Shades stilled in death, and tender twilight days
Ere Winter lifts the wind-trump to his lip.
No moss is shyly seen a tuft to raise,
Nor under grass a gold-eyed flower to dip;
Nor sound is breathed, but haply the south west
Faint rippling in the brushes of the pine,
Or of the shrunken leaf dry-fluttering.
Compact the village lies, a whitened line
Gathered in smoke. What holds this brooding rest?
Is it dead Autumn, or the dreaming Spring?

[75]

MAYFLOWERS

Where the dwarf pine reddens
The rocks and soil with its rusted leaves
    And skeleton cones;
    And the footstep deadens
As it clambers o'er roots and broken stones;   5
While a noise of waves the ear deceives
As the sigh of the wind through the foliage heaves,
    And the restless heart saddens
    With the surging tones;
      Where falls no change   10
From the best and brightest of spring tide hours,
And the children of Summer their gifts estrange
    When dashing with flowers
Lowland and upland and craggy range.
There, where Decay and chilled Life stared together   15
    Forlornly round,
In an April day of wilful weather,
The hidden Spring I found.

———

    Ere the Month in bays and hollows
      Strung with leaves the alder spray,   20
    Or with bloom on river-shallows,
      Dropped the wands of willows gray;

    Ere her fingers flung the cowslip
      Golden through the meadow-glade,
    Or the bloodroot's caps of silver   25
      Flickered where her feet had played;

19 *bays* LA *glades* 22 *Dropped* LA *Tipped* 23 *flung* ORIG:*flashed*
LA *raised* 24 *Golden through the meadow-glade,* LA *In the meadow sere*
and worn 26 *feet had played;* LA *steps had borne:*

[76]

Whilst above the bluffs were hiding
  Sullen brows in slouching snows,
Through the leaves my footstep sliding
  Fell where hers first touched and rose.   30

Underneath the dead pine droppings,
  Breaking white through mildewed mould,
Glimpsed a rosy chain of flowerets,
  Rosy flowerets fresh and cold:

Swept not, but by shadow swaying   35
  Of wild branch in windy air,
Couched the buds, unguessed and laying
  Star to star, in darkness there.

Eagerly, yet half reluctant,
  As the daylight lit on them,   40
Of its clinging tufts of odour
  Quick I stripped the trailing stem;

And their lights in cluster blending,
  Barren sounds and damp decays
Sank in sighs of Summer ending   45
  And a smell of balmy days.

So refreshed and fancy-solaced,
  Through the Shadow on I past,
While Life seemed to beat and kindle
  In the breath my darlings cast.   50

30 *Fell where hers first touched and rose* LA *Came where her first lights arose* 32 *Breaking white through mildewed* LA *Close entangled with the* 33 *Glimpsed* LA and ORIG:*Gleamed* 35 *Swept not, but by shadow swaying* LA *Shadowed, unwarmed by a breathing* 36 *Of wild branch in windy* LA *Softer than the northern* 37 *unguessed and laying* LA *their stars unsheathing* 38 *Star to star,* LA *Group by group* 43 *lights* LA *sweets* 44 *Barren* LA *Dreary* 45 *Sank in sighs of Summer* LA *Ceased, in summer murmurs* 48 *Shadow* LA *arches* 49 *beat* LA *throb*

As I parted from the pine trees,
   Gathering in as round a grave
Mourners close; above their branches,
   From a glimmering western cave,

Sunlight broke into the valley   55
   Filling with an instant glow
All its basin, from the brook bed
   To the dark edge touched with snow:

And by luring sweet and lustre,
   Summoned round those buds and me,   60
Red-ribbed leaf and starry cluster,
   Hurtled the bewildered bee.

So, until I found the village,
   Welcome glimmered in the air,
Where, from porch and vine-filled window,   65
   Beamed a welcome still more fair:

Girlish heads, half-seen and glancing,
   Peeped althrough the leaf lorn bowers;
And the little children, dancing,
   Clapped their hands and cried Mayflowers!   70

––––––––––

Since I found that buried garland,
   Fair and fresh and rosy-cold,
All has been its life foreshadowed;—
   Woods in umbrage banked and rolled,

   52 *Gathering in as round a grave* LA *Closing in a gloomy crowd;*
53 *Mourners close;* LA *O'er a swell,*   54 *a glimmering western cave,* LA *a
whitening western cloud*   57 *brook bed* LA *streamlet*   59 *luring sweet and*
ORIG: *flowers and loveliest*   60 *round those buds and me,*   ORIG: *from his
rock or tree*   61 *Red-ribbed leaf and starry* LA *Heavily about the*   ORIG:
Heavily round the   63 *So, until I found* LA *Thus, till round me stirred*
64 *glimmered* E *brightened*   67 *Girlish heads, half-seen and* LA *Rosy maids,
like wood-nymphs*   68 *althrough the leaf lorn* LA *amid the leafless*

Meadows brimmed with clover, ridges   75
    Where through fern the lupine crowds,
And upon the sandstone ledges
    Laurel heaped like sunset clouds.

But the wayward mind, regretful,
    Wanders through that April day,   80
And by fields forever faded
    Seems to tread a vanished way

Till it finds those low lights flushing
    Through the pine trees' mouldered spines,
And hears still the mournful gushing   85
    Of the north wind in the pines.

HYMN WRITTEN FOR THE DEDICATION
OF A CEMETERY

Beside the River's dark green flow,
    Here, where the pinetrees weep,
Red Autumn's winds will coldly blow
    Above their dreamless sleep:

Their sleep, for whom with prayerful breath   5
    We've put apart today
This spot, for shadowed walks of Death,
    And gardens of decay.

This crumbling bank with Autumn crowned,
    These pining woodland ways,   10
Seem now no longer common ground;
    But each in turn conveys

83 *low lights* ORIG: *blossoms*

12 *in turn* ORIG: *and all*

[79]

A saddened sense of something more:
    Is it the dying year?
Or a dim shadow, sent before,   15
    Of the next gathering here?

Is it that He, the silent Power,
    Has now assumed the place
And drunk the light of morning's hour,
    The life of Nature's grace?   20

Not so—the spot is beautiful,
    And holy is the sod;
'Tis we are faint, our eyes are dull;
    All else is fair in God.

So let them lie, their graves bedecked,   25
    Whose bones these shades invest,
Nor grief deny, nor fear suspect,
    The beauty of their rest.

INSPIRATION

The common paths by which we walk and wind
Unheedful, but perhaps to wish them done,
Though edged with brier and clotbur, bear behind
Such leaves as Milton wears or Shakespeare won.
Still, could we look with clear poetic faith,   5
No day so desert but a footway hath,
Which still explored, though dimly traced it turn,
May yet arrive where gates of glory burn:
Nay, scarce an hour of all the shining twelve

19 *drunk* MS *drank*

7 *turn* ORIG:*seem*   8 *burn* ORIG:*gleam*

[80]

But to the inmost sight may ope a valve 10
On those hid gardens where the great of old
Walked from the world and their sick hearts consoled
Mid bowers that fall not, wells which never waste,
And gathered flowers, the fruit whereof we taste:
While, of the silent hours that mourn the day, 15
Not one but bears a poet's crown away,
Regardless or unconscious how he might
Collect an import from the fires of night,
Which, when the hand is still, and fixed the head,
Shall tremble starlike o'er the undying dead; 20

 And, with a tearful glory,
  Through the darkness shadowing then,
 Still light the sleeper's story
  In the memories of men.

And such are mine: for me these scenes decay: 25
For me, in hues of change, are ever born
The faded crimson of a wasted day,
The gold and purple braveries of the morn,
The life of Spring, the strength that Summer gains,
The dying foliage sad September stains; 30
By latter Autumn shattered on the plain,
Massed by the wind, blent by the rotting rain;
Till belts of snow from cliff to cliff appear,
And whitely link the dead and newborn year.
All these, to music deep, for me unfold, 35
Yet vaguely die: their sense I cannot hold,
But shudder inly as the years drop by
And leave me lifting still a darkened eye.
Or if from these despondingly I go
To look for light where clear examples glow, 40

Though names constellate glitter overhead
To prompt the path and guide the failing tread,

20 *tremble* MS *glimmer* 37 *inly* E *darkly*

[81]

I linger, watching for a warmer gleam,
While still my spirit shivers and I seem

Like one constrained to wander   45
Alone till morning light,
Beneath the hopeless grandeur
Of a star-filled winter's night.

INFATUATION

'Tis his one hope: all else that round his life
So fairly circles, scarce he numbers now.
The pride of name, a lot with blessings rife,
Determined friends, great gifts that him endow,
Are shrunk to nothing in a woman's smile.   5
Counsel, reproof, entreaty, all are lost
Like windy waters which their strength exhaust,
And leave no impress; worldly lips revile
With sneer and stinging gibe, but idly by,
Unfelt, unheard, the impatient arrows fly: 10
Careless, he joins a parasitic train,
Fops, fools and flatterers whom her arts enchain,
Nor counts aught base that may to her pertain.
Immersed in love, or what he deems is such,
The present exigence he looks to please,   15
Nor seeks beyond, but only strives to clutch
That which will goad his heart but ne'er can ease:
As the drenched sailor, wrecked in Indian seas,
To some low reef of wounding coral clings
Mid slav'ry weed and drift and ocean scurf;   20
Yet heedeth not companionship of these,
But strains his quivering grasp and stoutly swings,
Despite of lifting swell and flinging surf.

18 *As* ᴇ *So*

[82]

SONNET

Again, again ye part in stormy grief
From these dark hills and bowers so built in vain,
And lips and hearts that will not move again,—
Pathetic Autumn and the writhled leaf;
Dropping away in tears with warning brief;
The wind reiterates a wailful strain,
And on the skylight beats the restless rain,
And vapor drowns the mountain, base and brow.
I watch the wet black roofs through mist defined,
I watch the raindrops strung along the blind,
And my heart bleeds, and all my senses bow
In grief; as one mild face with suffering lined
Comes up in thought: O wildly, rain and wind,
Mourn on; she sleeps, nor heeds your angry sorrow now.

PICOMEGAN

Stars of gold the green sod fretting,
Clemantis the thicket netting,
Silvery moss her locks down-letting
   Like a maiden brave:
Arrowhead his dark flag wetting   5
   In thy darker wave.

2 *dark* E *bare*   *so built in vain,* ORIG:*in ruin lain*   3 *move*   ORIG:*fade*
1 *green sod* P *greensward*

[83]

By the River's broken border
  Wading through the ferns,
When a darker deep, and broader,
  Fills its bays and turns: 10
Up along the winding ridges,
  Down the sudden-dropped descent,
Rounding pools with reedy edges,
  Silent coves in alders pent,
Through the river-flags and sedges   15
  Dreamily I went.

Dreamily, for perfect Summer
  Hushed the vales with misty heat;
In the wood a drowsy drummer,
  The woodpecker, faintly beat.   20
Songs were silent, save the voices
  Of the mountain and the flood,
Save the wisdom of the voices
  Only known in solitude:
But to me, a lonely liver,   25
  All that fading afternoon
From the undermining river
  Came a burthen in its tune,
Came a tone my ear remembers,
  And I said, "What grief thee grieves,   30
Pacing through thy leafy chambers,
  And thy voice of rest bereaves?
Winds of change that wail and bluster,
  Sunless morns and shivering eves,
Carry sweets to thee belonging;   35
  All of light thy rim receives:
River-growths that fold and cluster
  Following where the waters lead,
Bunches of the purple aster,
  Mints and blood-dropped jewelweed   40

30 *grief* P *is't* ORIG:*is it*

[84]

Like carnelians hanging
  'Mid their pale-green leaves;
Wherefore then with sunlight heaping
  Perfect joy and promised good,
When thy flow should pulse in keeping   45
  With the beating of the blood,
Through thy dim green shadows sweeping
When the folded heart is sleeping,
  Dost thou mourn and brood?"

Wider, wilder, round the headland,   50
  Black the River swung,
Over skirt and hanging woodland
  Deeper stillness hung;
As once more I stood a dreamer
  The waste weeds among: 55
Doubt, and pain, and grief extremer
  Seemed to fall away,
But a dim voluptuous sorrow
Smote and thrilled my fancy thoro',
  Gazing over bend and bay: 60
Saying, "Thou O mournful River
  As of old dost wind and waste,
Falling down the reef forever,
  Rustling with a sound of haste
Through the dry-fringed meadow bottom;   65
  But my hands aside thy bed
Gather now no gems of Autumn,
  Or the dainties Summer shed;
By the margin hoarsely flowing,
Yellow dock and garget growing,   70
Drifts of wreck and muddy stain,
By river-wash and dregs of rain.
Yet, though bound in desolation,
  Bound and locked, thy waters pour
With a cry of exultation   75

Uncontained by shore and shore,
With a booming deep vibration;
  In its wind my cheek is wet,
But unheeding woe or warning
  Thou through all the barren hours   80
  Seem'st to sing of Summer yet;
Thou with voice all sorrow scorning
  Babblest on of leaves and flowers,
Wearily, whilst I go mourning
  O'er thy fallen banks and bowers;   85
O'er a life small grace adorning,
  With lost aims and broken powers
Wreck-flung, like these wavetorn beaches,
  Tear trenched, as by winter showers.
But a faith thy music teaches   90
  Might I to its knowledge climb,
Still the yearning heart beseeches
  Truth, as when in summer time
Through these dells I vaguely sought her,
  In the dreamy summer time."   95
So the margin paths and reaches
  Once again I left to roam,
Left behind the roaring water,
  Eddy knots, and clots of foam;
But it still disturbed me ever,   100
  As a dream no reason yields,
From the ruin of the river,
  Winding up through empty fields,
That I could not gather something
  Of the meaning and belief,   105
In the voice of its triumphing
  Or the wisdom of its grief.

THE SUPERLATIVE

How strange a paradox is human life,
Strange in repose, yet stranger in its strife:
A walking dream, or fierce and barren toil,
A shifting fixture, an enduring change,
Tempting to baffle, promising to foil,   5
Strange in the garnered sum, and in the instance strange.

Strange that a man, whose soul the earthquake throb
Of Genius, like a buried Titan's sob,
Has lifted into stillness and sunshine,
Should, amid sordid fogs and earthly jars   10
That beat about his base, again decline
In place of gazing heaven, and striking to the stars.

Stranger that Woman, clad in sanctity
Of gentleness and love, with modesty
To guard her vesture like a golden zone,   15
Should rend away her robes, and shameless stand
In the world's eye, a wrangler, to disown
Her sex, and make it monstrous in an outraged land.

But strangest still, of these, or aught beside
Of human crime or folly, is the pride   20
Born of the gentlest gift we reach from Heaven;
Where hearts like these, stung by its bitterness,
Cease from each other, wild to be forgiven,
Yet proud to nurse an unrelenting wretchedness.

The stanzaic pattern is that of MS. In E the Alexandrines are not set into the margin.

The starry flower, the flowerlike stars that fade
And brighten with the daylight and the dark,
The bluet in the green I faintly mark,
Or glimmering crags with laurel overlaid,
Even to the Lord of light, the Lamp of shade,
Seem one to me, nor less divinely made
Than the crowned moon or heaven's great hierarch.
And so, dim grassy flower and night lit spark
Still move me on and upward for the True,
Seeking through change, growth, death, in new and old,
The full in few, the statelier in the less,
With patient pain; always remembering this:
His Hand, who touched the sod with showers of gold,
Stippled Orion on the midnight blue.

And so, as this great sphere now turning slow
Up to the light from that abyss of stars,
Now wheeling into gloom through sunset bars
With all its elements of form and flow,
And life in life; where crowned, yet blind doth go
The sensible king, is but an Unity
Compressed of motes impossible to know;
Which worldlike still in deep analogy
Have distance, march, dimension, and degree:
So the round earth which we the world do call
Is but a grain in that that mightiest swells,
Whereof the stars of light are particles,
As ultimate atoms of one infinite Ball
On which God moves and treads beneath his feet the All!

ʌ 4 *Or* E *And* 6 *Seem* E *Shine* *nor less divinely made* E *the least,
still glorious made* 7 *Than the crowned* E *As crowned*

ᵥ 5 *doth* E *must* 6 *an* E *a* 8 *Which* ORIG:*Yet still* E *yet* 9
distance, march ORIG:*order, place* 10 *round earth* ORIG:*vast whole* 13
As ORIG:*The*

THE QUESTION

How shall I array my love?
How should I arrange my fair?
Leave her standing white and silent
In the richness of her hair?
Motion silent, beauty bare   5
In the glory of her hair?
Or, for place and drapery,
Ravage land, and sack the sea?

Or from darkest summer sky,
When the white belts, riding high,   10
Cut the clear like ribs of pearl,
On the eastern upland's curl,
In the time of dusk and dew
Tear away a breadth of blue?
Touched from twilight's rosy bars,   15
With each twinkling tuft of stars,
And, shaking out the glints of gold,
Catch her softly from the cold?
Catch and lift her to the cloud,
Where to crown her, passing proud,   20
Gliding, glistening woods of June
Reach the rain-ring from the moon?

Or to fold her warmer wise
Let me try in garb and guise
Gathered from this mortal globe;   25
Roll her beauty in a robe
Of the Persian lilach stain,
Purple, dim with filigrane:
Belted in with rarer red
Than India's leaf ere figured,   30

21 *glistening*   ORIG: *glimmering*

[89]

Put a crown upon her head.
Then to lead her high and cold
Where, from a step of silver rolled,
A crimson floweth on the floor
Like a river riding o'er 35
Pearl and priceless marbles bright,
Onyx, myrrhine, marcasite,
And jasper green: nor these alone,
But the famed Phengites stone,
And leading upward to the throne. 40
Prop and pillar, roof and rise,
All ashake with drops and dyes
And the diamond's precious eyes;
And she, as if a sudden storm
Had fallen upon her face and form; 45
Diamonds like raindrops rare,
Pearls like hailstones in her hair;
In the lamplight's ruddy stream
Jewels crossed with jewels gleam
On jewels, jewel-circled there; 50
While round her wrists and ankles bare
Gems of jewels glimpse and gaze,
Hyacinth, rose-stone, idocrase.

Or she stealeth, soft arrayed
Like a white Haemonian maid, 55
Winding under cypress shade,
Cedar shade and paths of green
With porch and pillar white between:
Amaranth eyes do mine behold,
Hair like the pale marigold: 60
Dreamily she seems to me
Hero or Herodice!
With a sidelong motion sweet,
Thoro' flowers she draws her feet;

53 *rose-stone* ORIG: *amianth*

[90]

This way now the ripples come,   65
Shower myrtles, myrrh, and gum
With heliochryse and amomum.

Ah! not so, New England's flower,
Separate must her beauty be
From stars of old mythology: 70
Priestesses, or Crysophorae;
Nor fairy garb nor kingly dower
May fit her in her radiant hour;
Free and bold her steps must flow,
All men see her come and go;   75
At her feet the planet lies,
Day and night are in her eyes,
Over her the star-flag strewn:
Lo! she standeth there alone,
Pride, in her dark glances, king,   80
Love, her cheek rose-coloring:
In a garden all her own,
Lo, she standeth, crowned on
With rare roses, round her drawn
Texture like the webs of dawn   85
On the rosebeds lingering,
While my heart to her I bring;
Heart and garden all her own—
What in truth cares such a one
Though my arm could round her throw   90
Gleam of gods, or crowns bestow?
Or though the old gods could confer
All godlike gifts and grace on her?
The young Medusa's locks divine,
Pelops' shoulder eburnine,   95
Lips that drew the Ismenean bees,
Tears of the Heliades
Dropped into glimmering shells that be

74 *bold*   ORIG:*fair*   98 *glimmering*   E *shimmering*

[91]

About the indraught of the sea:
The river-riches of the sphere,   100
All that the dark sea bottoms bear,
The wide earth's green convexity,
The inexhaustible blue sky,
Hold not a prize, so proud, so high
That it could grace her, gay or grand,   105
By garden-gale and rosebreath fanned;
Or as tonight I saw her stand
Lovely in the meadow land
With a clover in her hand.

Twilight

I

In the darkening silence
When the hilltops dusk and fail,
And the purple damps of evening now
No longer edge the vale:
When the faint flesh-tinted clouds have parted   5
To the westward, one by one,
In the glimmering silence,
I love to steal alone
By river and by runside,
Through knots of aspens gray,   10
And hearken for the voices
Of a music ceased away.

109: *clover*. In the margin of ms, Tuckerman admonished the printer
not to print "cleaver"!

In ms the last four lines of each stanza are written as two. In the margin
Tuckerman wrote a note to the printer, directing him to "print these two
last lines as four, throughout the piece—making 12 lines for a verse."

[92]

About the winding water
And among the bulrush spears,
Like the wind of empty Autumn, comes   15
Their sorrow in my ears.
Like the wind of hollow Autumn blowing
   From swamp and shallow dim,
   Comes the sorrow of the voices;
   Whilst along the weedy brim   20
   I follow in the evenfall,
   And darkly reason why
Those whispers breathe so mournfully
   From depths of days gone by.

III

Is it that in the stealing   25
   Of the tender tearful tones,
   The knowledge stirs that bowers and homes
   Are dust and fallen stones
Where once they sang? that on lips so loving
   Settled a still gray sleep,   30
   With tears, though mindful memory
   Still brings them from the deep?
   Is it that Conscience muses,
   " 'Twas for thee their deep hearts heaved?"
   Or is it so, that I am not   35
   What those best hearts believed?

IV

O falling stream, O voices,
   O grief, O gaining night,
   Ye bring no comfort to the heart:
   Ye but again unite   40

34 *deep* ᴇ *high*

[93]

In a brooding gloom, and a windy wail;
    And a sorrow cold like Death
    Steals from the river-border,
    Falls in the dampening breath
    Of the unavailing night wind,   45
    Falls with the strength of tears,
    And an unreal bitterness
    On the life of latter years.

                    v

    I see the flags of the River
    And the moss-green alder bark,   50
    While faintly the far-set village lights
    Flash through the rainy dark:
And the willow drops to the dipping water,
    But why, from shelf and shore,
    Comes the trouble of the voices   55
    Of the loved of heretofore?
    They never knew these shadows;
    And the river's sighing flow
    Swept not their ears in those dim days,
    Nor lulled them long ago.   60

                    VI

    Sunk are the ships, or shattered,
    Yet amid the burying foam,
    On the wild sea-bar, glance here and there,
    As the surges go and come,
Pieces and parts of a broken vessel: 65
    So to this stranger stream
    And its still woods, come thronging in,
    Thought, memory, doubt, and dream
    Of the noble hearts that sailed with me;

47 *an unreal* ORIG:*unmeaning* 62 *amid* E *as 'mid* 63 *glance* ORIG:
gleam E *beat* 67 *thronging* E *drifting*

Here to this desert spot   70
Come their dim ghosts, where they indeed
Were known and nurtured not.

VII

'Tis the heart, the heart remembers
And with wild and passionate will,
Peoples the woods and vales, and pours   75
Its cry round stream and hill.
I look o'er the hills to the mournful morning,
    And it whispers still of home,
    And in the darkening of the day
Impels me forth to roam   80
With a desolate and vague desire,
    Like the evil spirit's quest
    Who walketh through dry places
Seeking still, nor finding rest.

VIII

Yet, in the gathering silence,   85
When the hilltops fade and fail,
And the tearful tints of twilight now
No longer edge the vale;
When the crimson-faded clouds have parted
    To the westward, one by one,   90
    In the passionate silence
I love to steal alone
By river and by runside,
    Through knots of aspens gray,
    And hearken for the voices   95
Of a music ceased away.

86 *fade*   E *faint*

ELIDORE

Her beauty came to his distrustful heart
As comes a bud to flower in bracing air;
For its perception had been dulled to sleep
By disappointment, doubt, and worldly wear,
The fear of wrong, and coldness everywhere: 5
Yet, while unguessed, an impulse seemed to part
From that pale presence, calling him to keep
A watch on Beauty's beamings, powers, and tones:
From blossoming dawn down to the half-filled flower,
Or bird, or buried book: all that Life owns   10
Or Nature gives, grew holier in that power.

An influence still entreating, day by day,
Yet still unlike the tricks of female guile,
Not forward, but to touch and reconcile
Through childlike warmth and plain sincerity;   15
And teaching him by such innocence of display
That light of outward loveliness to see.
Scarce felt at first, with Time's increasing worth
The faint eyes deepened and the lips awoke,
Till from a clouded brow all beauty broke,   20
And bade him own a wonder of the earth,
A graceful mind most gracefully inclosed:
A woman fair and young, but softly free
From the world's wisdom and hypocrisy,
Or restless spite or curiosity: 25
Gentle and glad, yet armed in constancy,
With breathings heavenward and a faith composed.

---

4 *worldly* E *wordly* 8 *beamings* ORIG:*gleamings* 14 *touch* E *reach*
15 *warmth* E *grace*

[96]

Such is the Beauty dowered not to deceive;
Such *was* the Beauty that dispersed his fear
And smiled, and said, "O world-sick heart believe!"   30
Doubting, he saw all doubts and bodings grim,
Like night dissolving, break and disappear,
While Joy and Trust relumed his vision dim:
Such Joy as clears the woodlost wanderer's sight,
Who, pushing darkly on with body bowed,   35
Through trunks and brush discerns a peering light,
And sees it shine, a star of safety soon:
Or like a stormy moonrise, when the moon
Grows from some blackened ridge of thundercloud,
And slow perfects herself in wondering eyes   40
That brighten with her round: so sweet surprise
Brightened his look as that strange beauty beamed
To illume a heart, that had its grace, its power, misdeemed.

THE CLEARING

Here, where the River wheels
    Through countries called the midland,
Of this fair tract, the flower and crown,
    Once stood a wild of woodland:
But now no belt of brown   5
    Beech, alder, ash, or oaken,
Is left: and Autumn's Lamp reveals
    All barren, bald, and broken.

A slope of rugged marl—
    For copse and dreamy dingle,   10
The larches burned, the birches flayed,
    Or gone for beam and shingle:
The beeches in whose shade
    The hunter shaped his paddle,
With scrawly bush and brushwood-snarl,   15
    Have vanished, stock and staddle.

[97]

Beside the Run whose flow
    The season touched with flowers,
Or softly staunched with fallen leaves,
    Or fed with perfumed showers,   20
A shirt with tattered sleeves
    Slaps in the gust of summer,
And dimly, soapy breathings blow
    Across the vagrant roamer.

Here, where the golden grace   25
    Of moonlight fell in shatters,
By dark, a dingy, flickering line
    Frets on the tossing waters:
For here, where then the pine
    Tanned with his droppings scanty   30
This rock, the Poet's resting-place
    Is propt, an Irish shanty.

O not upon the edge
    Of grove, or ranging river,
At eve, or in the general day,   35
    Where'er thy steps endeavor,
Shall thee such rest delay,
    O dreamer in the Shadow—
By axe and beetle, blast and wedge,
    Now torn from marge and meadow;   40

Thou, whom no sorrow sears,
    Nor sour mischances harden,
Will seek no more the pitcher plant
    To deck thy slender garden,
In this thy holy haunt: 45
    Gone are the happy bowers,
And thou apart in other years
    Must rove for other flowers.

23 *dimly*   E *vaguely*   27 *flickering*   ORIG:*glimmering*   43 *Will*   E *Wilt*

The Spring wind will not come
　　Now like a pleasant rumor,　　　　　　　　　　50
Nor the sultry song of harvest-fly
　　To sting the ear of Summer.
And when the woods are dry,
　　Or red with Autumn's dawning,
This bay will miss a music from　　　　　　　　　55
　　Dim arch or crimson awning;

Yet when November rains
　　Shall settle on the forest,
And wash the color from the wood,
　　His darlings from the florist,　　　　　　　　60
'Twill seem a glimpse of good,
　　A compensation tender,
Remembering that to this remains
　　No beauty now to render;

And that, for what we love,　　　　　　　　　　65
　　Though doubt and dread benumb us,
The gracious Past, the yielded boon,
　　Can ne'er be taken from us:
Then let us hold what's gone—
　　And hug each greener minute,　　　　　　　　70
Though shanties smoke in every cove
　　And Paddies rule the senate;

Yes, though for belt and bower
　　The hard dry tangle bristles,
And the bloomy hollows swarm and burn　　　　　75
　　With tickseed, tares, and thistles,
And the River runs forlorn—
　　We go not unrequited,
Whilst memory glasses heaven and flower
　　Wherein our love delighted.　　　　　　　　80

51 *sultry*　E *long hot*

[99]

And may this Picture gay,
   Deep rooted in my bosom,
The blue above forever seal,
   Forever shade the blossom
Unswept by worldly steel   85
   Or Sorrow's fire and powder,
Give lordlier off the limb, and sway
   The surgy summit prouder.

But if through bough and butt,
   Time's dull steel chops and craunches   90
And lumber lies for noble stems,
   And wreck for wreathing branches,
And all the glory dims—
   May I, for deep-loved Nature,
Though brute his being, and base his hut,   95
   Replace it with the Creature.

To the River

'Tis nearly night: a healing night,
   As Carro's words last-spoken,
And will the day be blue and bright?
   A whole bright day unbroken?
You ask of me, who walk to learn,   5
   Regardless wealth amassing,
And take no charge of tide or turn,
   And scarcely keep, in passing,

A watch on wind and weather-gleam:
   Of these things no recorder,   10
Yet o'er the dark I almost seem
   To see its golden border.
Behind the night is hid the day—
   I cannot find the reason

In rule or rhyme, but all things say   15
    'Twill be a day of season.

And Carro too will softer smile,
    And Carro's frown be rarer,
But leave your fair a little while,—
    You'll find her all the fairer,—   20
To walk with me; not by the road,
    A little breathing give her,
And we will keep the winding wood
    Until we strike the River.

And I will tell where Love, though loath,   25
    A fuller harvest heapeth
Than yours, yet I have known the growth,
    And followed where he reapeth;
And this, though now to heaven you cast,
    Appealing, death-defiant,   30
A passion pitiless and vast
    As love of god or giant!

For one is beat with blasting tears,
    And burned with raging weather,
And reapt in fiery haste, the ears   35
    Half-ripe, deadripe or neither:
The other hangs with dim rain prest,
    All greenly wet, and groweth
Forever in the realms of rest,
    Nor end nor seedtime knoweth.   40

Yet some, who cannot help to see,
    Refuse the day, and many,
Where faintest strokes of sunlight be,
    Peep hard for pin and penny,

25 *Love* ORIG:*Thou loath,* MS *loth*   26 *A fuller harvest heapeth*
ORIG:*Love, a burthen reapest*   27 *Than yours* ORIG:*More deep*   28 *fol-*
lowed where he reapeth ORIG:*strode in it at deepest*   31 *passion pitiless*
ORIG:*Love implacable*   32 *love of god or* ORIG:*gods, or god-born*

[101]

Who sneer at what the meadow spreads   45
    And what the woods environ,
And, like the sons of Use, with heads
    And hands and feet of iron

Would grasp the Titan's scythe to wound,
    To sweep the hill asunder.   50
And shear the groves at one swing round
    And tread the Muses under:
Yet still best-pleased amid the roar,
    I find myself a debtor,
Love men not lesser than before,   55
    And Nature more than better.

There be, with brains no folding shroud
    Of grief can wean or widow
Of vacant mirth, who bear the cloud,
    Yet shrink from shade of shadow: 60
Would flit forever in the shine,
    Despite of burns and blisters,
And add another to the Nine,
    More foolish than her sisters:

A denary of graceful girls   65
    That carol, dance, and sidle
Through chaffering crowds and giddying whirls
    Of life, all loud and idle.
But I, who love the graver Muse,
    And Minna more than Brenda,   70
Walk not with these, nor find my views
    Writ down in their credenda.

Why, for some peep of meaning clear,
    Should we ourselves deliver
Up to the stream, which even here   75
    Roars past us like a River?

73 *peep* ORIG:*glimpse*   76 *Roars* ORIG:*Runs*

[102]

But bend and let the hurly pass,
  Pedant and fop, chance-hitters!
Whilst in the fields of faded grass
  The cricket ticks and twitters;   80

With those that loose the languid page,
  Nor let the life o'erflow it,
But pick and copy, sap and sage,
  Part wit, and parcel poet;
They follow fast some empiric,   85
  Nor heed for watch or warden,
But go in crowds and settle thick
  Like crows in Nature's garden.

They chew the sweet, and suck the sour,
  And know not which is sweeter,   90
The cowslip and calypso flower,
  Bald-breath, and burning metre,
Milton or Skelton, all is one—
  None darkle dim where none shine—
And with a blindness of their own   95
  They blot the breeze and sunshine.

O might I plunge beneath the flow
  For one forgetful minute,
And, leaving all my dreams below,
  Rise like a bubble in it,   100
And sweep along to lose myself
  With all the current seizes;
But in the blows of brass and delf
  I fear to go to pieces;

Perhaps my hand would urge the cup   105
  To press apart a nation,
Or where the fountain forces up
  Drop tears of congelation:

94 *darkle* ORIG:*glimmer* 95 *blindness* ORIG:*darkness* 105 *urge*
ORIG:*push*

[103]

Or pull with them that strain to drag
 The chords of Union tauter,   110
Stream to the polls with club and flag,
 And crossed with sacred water.

But hold: nor cloud our night with these;
 Why should we crowd or quarrel?
Look! in the west the Golden Bees   115
 Hang o'er the mountain laurel:
And see, in every spot of wet
 The coltsfoot groups and glistens,
While with a dew, the holiest yet,
 Young Night her children christens.   120

Why should I set my feeble strength
 A bitter blame to cancel,
Or hold a traitor up at length,
 Or tear away a tinsel,
Or beat about for bribe or boon   125
 When here, in pool and shallow,
I see the fragment of a moon,
 Rimmed with a fragment halo?

A SOUL THAT OUT OF NATURE'S DEEP

A soul that out of Nature's deep
 From inner fires had birth;
Yet not as rocks or rosebuds peep:
 Nor came it to the earth,

A drop of rain at random blown,   5
 A star point burning high,
Lit in the dark, and as alone
 As Lyra in the sky:

111 *polls* MS *poles* 118 *groups* ORIG:*gleams*

[104]

Nor ushered in with stormy air,
 Sea shock, or earthquake jars,   10
Nor born to fame beneath some rare
 Conspiracy of stars;

Nor fortune-crowned with benefits:
 The life was larger lent,
Made up of many opposites   15
 In contradiction blent:

A nature affable and grand,
 Yet cold as headland snow,
Large-handed, liberal to demand,
 Though still to proffer slow;   20

That shunned to share the roaring cup,
 The toast and cheerings nine,
Nor cared to sit alone to sup
 The pleasure of the wine;

Yet genial oft by flash and fit—   25
 High manners, courage mild—
God gave him these and savage wit
 Yet like an Indian child:

He held from Nature's self indeed
 The wisdom to descry   30
A weathercock in the waving weed,
 A clock face in the sky.

But he, amid these bowers and dales
 A larger import drew,
Beneath more cordial sunlight, gales,   35
 And skies of sounder blue,

28 *Yet like* ᴇ *As to*   29 *He held from Nature's self* ᴇ *And gave him*
more than this   34 *import* ᴇ *life-breath*   35 *sunlight* ᴇ *sunshine*

[105]

Than only this. Beside the brook,
　　With far forgetful eye,
Or toward the deep hills would he look,
　　Watching the daylight die;　　　　　　　　　40

Brooding in dim solicitude
　　On earlier other times
And yon dark-purple wing of wood
　　That o'er the mountain climbs;

And fancies thick like flowerbuds bright,　　　　45
　　Rare thoughts in affluence rank,
Came at the onset of the light,
　　Nor with the sunset sank.

He slept not, but the dream had way,
　　And his watch abroad was cast　　　　　　50
With the earliest light of the earliest day;
　　And when the light fell fast,

He stood in the river-solitudes
　　To mark the daylight go,
And low in the dusk of the wailing woods　　　55
　　He heard the nighthawk blow:

The nighthawk and the whippoorwill
　　Across the plashes dim,
Calling her mate from bower and hill,
　　Made prophecy for him:　　　　　　　　60

The nighthawk and the bird bereaved,
　　His airy calendars,
He stood till night had, unperceived,
　　Surrounded him with stars.

37 *only this*　ORIG:*wait on all*　40 *daylight*　E *glory*

[106]

O dear the look of upward eyes   65
    Lifted in love and light,
A smile to bless and humanize
    A hand to fold aright;

A silver voice to lead and lull;
    Slight step, and streamy hair,   70
But O! she was too beautiful
    That he should call her fair.

A love to pay, a life to give,
    Was hers; for this she strove:
And he too loved and would not live   75
    To live out of her love.

And childhood came his smile beneath
    And lingered hour on hour
With sweepy lids and innocent breath
    Like the grape-hyacinth flower: 80

For this, for all, his heart was full—
    Yet to the deeper mind
All outward passion seemed to dull
    That inmost sense refined

That broods and feeds where few have trod,   85
    And seeks to pass apart,
Imaging nature, man and God,
    In silence in the heart.

He saw, for to that secret eye
    God's hidden things were spread,   90
The wiser world in darkness lie,
    And Faith by Falsehood led.

Virtue and Envy, side by side:
    Blind Will that walks alone,

66 *in love and light*   E *with pleading might*

[107]

And mighty throngs that come and glide,   95
    Unknowing and unknown;

Great lights but quenched: strength, foresight, skill,
    Gone without deed or name,
And happy accidents that still
    Misplace the wreaths of fame;   100

Religion, but a bruited word
    'Twixt men who difference view
Between our Saviour, God the Lord,
    And Jesus Christ the Jew!

Yet unto all one wall and fold,   105
    One bed that all must share,
The miser brooding holy gold,
    The fool and spendthrift heir;

Still through the years the wrinkled chuff
    Acre to acre rolled: 110
And he too will have land enough
    When his mouth is filled with mould.

And vaster visions did he win
    From cloud and mountain bars,
And revelations that within   115
    Fell like a storm of stars!

Yet checked and crossed by doubt and night:
    Dim gulfs and solitudes
Of the deep mind; or warmth and light
    Broke from its shifting moods,   120

As when in many-weathered March
    Maybuds break up through snow,
And, spilt like milk, beneath the larch
    The little bluets blow;

Beneath the lilac and the larch   125
    In many a splash and spot;
Nor belting sea, nor Heaven's blue arch,
    Bound in where these were not

With Love and Peace: yet strangely sank
    Cold sorrow on his soul,   130
For human wisdom and the blank
    Summation of the whole.

Nor seemed it fit that one, unnerved
    And faint, should rouse the earth
Or build with those whose zeal had served   135
    But to incense his mirth.

Troubled to tears he stood and gazed,
    Unknowing where to weep,
To spend his cries o'er fabrics razed,
    Or a safe silence keep;   140

Renouncing human life and lore,
    Love's calm, and love's excess,
Experience and allegiance, for
    A higher passiveness.

So to drink full of Nature, much   145
    Recipient, still to woo
Her windy walk where pinetrees touch
    Against the ribby blue;

To find her feet by singing rills,
    Adoring and alone,   150
O'er grassy fields, to the still hills,
    Her solemn seat and throne!

130 *Cold* ORIG:*Dark*   144 *higher* ORIG:*wiser*

Sore struggle! yet, when passed, that seemed
    A crowning victory o'er
Himself and human bands: he deemed   155
    The battle more and more,

And like that warfare urged upon
    Unkingly lust and ease,
Which the fifth Henry waged and won;
    Or that Lydiades   160

Who left his looser life with tears,
    And in the fire of youth
Grew grave and chaste, Arcadian years,
    And reigned, kings, heroes both.

Ah, so—but not to him returned,   165
    Our monarch, meed like this,
But darker kin his grief had spurned,
    And bitter friends were his.

Distrust and Fear beside him took,
    With Shame, their hateful stands: 170
And Sorrow passed, and struck the book
    Of knowledge from his hands.

He saw, with absent sorrowing heed,
    All that had looked so fair;
His secret walk was waste with weed,   175
    His gardens washed and bare.

The very woods were filled with strife:
    Fierce beaks and warring wings
Clashed in his face; the heart and life
    Of those deep-hidden springs   180

153 *passed* MS *past*   154 *victory* E *conquest*   156 *battle* E *victory*
163 *Grew* E *Lived*   167 *darker* E *sterner*   169 *Fear* MS *fear*   171
passed MS *past*   175 *waste* E *wild*   176 *washed* ORIG:*wrecked*

No more his spirit cared to quaff:
  Great Nature lost her place,
Pushed from her happy heights, and half
  Degraded of her grace.

And so he saw the morning white   185
  As eyes with tears opprest,
The last heart-breaking gleam of light
  That dies along the West:

And so he saw the opening flower
  Dry in the August sheaf,   190
And on green Summer's top and tower,
  Only the turning leaf:

For Summer's darkest green, explored,
  Betrays the crimson blight,
As, in the heart of darkness cored,   195
  Red sparks and seeds of light

And lightning lurk, ready to leap
  Abroad, beyond reclaim,
To bathe a world in splendour deep,
  Or snatch in folding flame.   200

He saw, with manners, age and mode,
  Opinion rise and sink,
The jarring clash of creed and code,
  And knew not what to think:

Beliefs of ritual and of race;   205
  And hard it was to tell
Why good should come by gift of grace,
  And wrong be chargeable.

Before him burned attainless towers:
  Behind, a comfortless   210
Dim valley, dark with poison flowers
  And weeds of barrenness.

209 *burned* ORIG:*gleamed* 211 *dark* E *waste*

[111]

The early light, the early dream,
　　Had vanished; faint and chill
Like morning's, did the sunlight stream　　　　　215
　　On woodland, house and hill:

Yet, as of old, he ranged apart
　　By river-bank and bed,
And mused in bitterness of heart;
　　And to himself he said,　　　　　220

"Tear sullen Monkshood where he stands
　　Tall by the garden walk,
With burning pricks and venom glands
　　Beat down the nettle's stalk:

Lobelia from the margin break,　　　　　225
　　With Arum's blistering bell;
And over all let the bundle reek
　　With the smilax' loathly smell.

Fools' parsley from the graves of fools
　　With deadly darnels bring,　　　　　230
Yew, garget, dogwood of the pools
　　And the fen's unwholesome spring;

And laurel pull, and strip from trees
　　Of cypress red-bud rare,
And hemlock; but prick in with these　　　　　235
　　The shaft of a lily fair;

And bind them up, rank blossom, sting,
　　Bough, berry, poison-rife,
Embodying and embleming
　　The gleanings of a life."　　　　　240

213 *light* E *ray* 215 *morning's* E *winter sunlight* E *morning*
224 *Beat down* E *Pluck off* 225 *margin* E *rivage* 228 *loathly* MS
horrible 231 *of* ORIG:*from* 233 *laurel* E *hemlock strip* E *snatch*
trees E *bees* 234 *Of cypress* E *Half-drugged,* MS *Of cypress and* 235
hemlock E *laurel* 236 *fair;* MS *fair."* 238 *Bough,* ORIG:*Bur* 240
life." MS *life.*

[112]

Yet was not she, the lily flower,
   'Mid failings and misdeeds,
The fruit of many a scattered hour,
   Yet fairer for the weeds?

And was she not, through shade and shower,   245
   In patient beauty drest,
Though lonely in her place and power,
   Enough to save the rest?

Perhaps: yet darker gloomed the vale
   And dawned the turrets fair,   250
Beyond the height of ladder's scale
   Or any step of stair:

And yearned his soul for sharper change
   And knowledge of the light;
Yet not by station, staff, or range   255
   Of human toil or flight

Would he ascend: choosing alone
   With grief to make his bed
Like those whose godhead is their own,
   On whom the curse is said—   260

Who kindle to themselves a fire,
   And in the light thereof
Walk and are lost: but his desire
   Was still for wiser love,

And sought but in the holy place,   265
   And scarcely sought but found
In still reception: failing this
   All life in death seemed drowned.

250 *dawned*   ORIG:*gleamed*

Yet sometimes, doubting, discord-tost,
　　Came voices to his side:　　　　　　　　　　270
Echoes of youth, and friendships lost,
　　Or lost, or left aside.

Faces, wherein deep histories are,
　　Began to float and flee
And hover darkly, like a far　　　　　　　　　275
　　Forgotten memory;

Dim gardens, where a silent creek
　　Stole onward, margin-mossed;
And walks with here and there a streak
　　Of dusky odour crossed,　　　　　　　　　　280

Stirring the wells of tears: he saw
　　The vision of his youth
With holy grief, with holy awe:
　　The temple towers of Truth

Broke nearer; like a thunder-flash　　　　　　285
　　Again came back the dream
And light in many a bar and dash,
　　Like moonlight, flake and beam—

Or when dark clouds of middle air
　　Through hurrying gaps reveal　　　　　　　290
Arcturus, or the sailing star
　　That spurs Orion's heel:

Heaven's lights! yet covered as we look;
　　So momently to view
Came back the sparkle of the brook　　　　　295
　　And fields his childhood knew.

---

275 *hover* ORIG:*glimmer*　288 *flake and beam* ORIG:*break and gleam*
289 *dark* E *wild*

Fair faith and love with peace almost;
　　Yet, in that light serene,
He saw only a glory lost,
　　And what he might have been.　　　　　300

The precious grains his hands had spilled
　　Had fallen to others; they
Had passed before, his place was filled,
　　And the world rolled away:

Too late he learned that Nature's parts,　　305
　　Whereto we lean and cling,
Change, but as change our human hearts,
　　Nor grow by worshipping;

And that her presence, fair or grand
　　In these faint fields below,　　　　　310
Importeth little, seen beyond
　　Our welfare or our woe:

Nor good from ill can we release,
　　But weigh the world in full,
Not separate taken, part and piece,　　　315
　　But indiscerptible.

In law and limit tempests blow:
　　Tides swing from shore to shore,
And so the forest tree will grow
　　As grew the tree before.　　　　　　320

Too late he learned by land and sea
　　This bitter truth to glean:
That he who would know what shall be
　　Must ponder what hath been;

Nor unto fear of falsehood yield　　　　325
　　His strength, the good to balk,

Nor fold his arms beside the field,
  But *with* the furrow walk

Ready to cast his grain: and slower
  To faint, more credulous,   330
Believing well that but by our
  Own hands God helpeth us.

And who would find out Wisdom's grot
  To make her footsteps his,
Must learn to look where it is not   335
  As well as where it is.

THE STRANGER

Ere the first red-orange glimmer
  Touched the dial on the lawn,
In the earliest shade and shimmer
    Of the dawn:
When the dark was growing dimmer,   5
  And the moon, 'mid wavy clouds
Struggling for the horizon land,
  Had vanished like a worn out swimmer:
Feeding on the misty shrouds,
  Nature's grief to grief suborning,   10
Stood a man alone in sorrow
  On a lifted ledge of pines;
Over mounted woods and sand,
  Valley, and rolling mountain lines,
Watching for the morrow: 15
  Watching for the daylight,
In the weeping twilight,
  In the anguish of the morning.

When first I paused upon these barren bluffs
Of westland Massachusetts, and looked off   20
From mountain-roofs thatched by the dropping pine
With his loose leaf, a natural water-shed:
Upon the hamlet twinkling through the growth,
The river-silver scattered in the grass,
And all the Tyrian hills, there seemed to me   25
No spot so fair in all the fair Estate.
And he believed it too, for when the hours
Had field by field unlinked the folded vale,
And led me softly by the mountain paths,
And up the hollow rivers; teaching still   30
New names and natures in their tangled round;
And I had followed all the groves that go
From Shaking Acres to the Neighbor's Hole!
Still, with each deep-blue gap, or piece of pines,
Or upland farmfield lovely and apart,   35
I found him there, the Stranger. Vague and dim
The wind stirs through these mountain-terraces
In the turning day; and such his motion seemed:
Yet, like the ailing wind, went everywhere
With a faint fluttering step; and when he stood,   40
He stood as one about to fall, as now
Sick Autumn stands, with weak-blue vapour crowned.
A man who seemed to have walked through life alone:
Feeble he was, and something stepped in years,
Yet sought no succour save of sun and shade: 45
But ever went apart and held his face
Deep in the shadow: but most he loved to lie
By poplar shafts, or where yon maple stock
Bears on his fork a ball of umbrage up
And waits for Autumn's wain: in the deep day,   50
At morning's edge, or night, his place was there.

23 *twinkling*   ORIG:*glimmering*   31 *tangled*   E *thoughtful*   44 *he was,*
ORIG:*at that*

[117]

Skirting the valley, north by needle runs
A sapling-coppice, scrags and second-growth,
With sucker brush and seedlings intermixed,
And a wood path thrids through from end to end.   55
There droops the scented pyrola, and there
The perfect fragrance of the partridge flower:
'Mid moss and maiden-hair and damp dead leaves,
A poet's cloister for a hidden hour.
And there I found him murmuring to himself   60
Like a low brook, but could not come to drink
His words; for still the bond that should have drawn
Held us apart, that love of lonely Nature,
And quick impatience of human neighborhood.
And I believed he was some natural poet,   65
With a great sorrow hard against his heart,
And shunned to tread too close: yet while I looked
On the sad patient brow and the fixed lip
Where silence brooded, I longed to look within
On the completed story of his life;   70
So easy still it seemed to lift the hand,
And open it, as I would a disused door
Locked with a dusty web: but he passed out;
And if he had a grief it went with him,
And all the treasure of his untold love;   75
A love that carried him forward with the cloud,
Drew him with river-currents, and at night
Impelled him to the mountain's edge and fall
Among the crowding woods and cataracts.
                                        So
The summer parted: but ere Autumn's cold   80
Bade the fall-cricket cease his mournful hymn,
By steps and rests of rock, I once again,
Half seeking him I shunned, one still fair day
And in the sunshine of the afternoon,
Climbed upward to the overlooking ledge   85
And stood in thought beneath the dropping pine.

56 *droops* E *breathes* 67 *looked* E *gazed* 80 *but* ORIG:*yet*

There shook the shining River, and there glimpsed
The village sunk in foliage at my feet,
And one vast pine leaned outward to the gulf.
On a great root that held the tree to the hill   90
I saw him sitting, till the late red light
Fell wearing westward, and still he sat and looked
Toward the dim remainder of the day;
And in his hand a bunch of blazing leaves,
Torn from the sumach as he passed along;   95
While round his feet gathered the mountain flower,
Dry asters, hardhack, and the withering fern:
The night came dark between us on the hill,
And nevermore have I beheld his face;
Yet often since, when I have walked with Sorrow,   100
In solitude, and hopelessness of heart,
Have I recalled that time, and wondered whether
The old man still went weary on the earth,
And if my dreams of his high gift were true.
But I have waited long indeed to hear   105
These rivers break in song, or, bluely dark,
Behold these mountains rank in rolling verse,
Or our red forests light the landscape line:
Something I still have learned,—respect of patience,
And the mysterious Will that proves the heart,   110
Breaking away the blossoms of its joy,
And for our latest love, restoring grief:
A swifter sympathy for human pain,
And knowledge of myself grown out of this,
Unguessed before: a humbler higher belief   115
In God and Nature, and more surrendered love.
Still clings the pine root clamped into the crag,
But the dead top is dry, beneath whose boughs
He sat and watched the west; and in my walks
So changed I feel as I approach the place,   120
So old in heart and step, it almost seems

---

87 *shook the shining* MS *radiated the* ORIG:*shook the glimmering*
glimpsed ORIG:*gleamed* 92 *wearing* ORIG:*waning*

[119]

As if the Wanderer left his life for mine
When night came dark between us on the hill:
A double interchange, as if indeed
'Twas my old self that disappeared with him,   125
And he in me still walks the weary earth.
But these are fancies, and so indeed is most
That I have thought or uttered in this regard,
Worthless of utterance maybe at the best,
Since first the Stranger came among these rocks: 130
A common man perhaps, with common cares,
Guiltless of grief, or high romantic love
Of natural beauty; a common life at last,
Though strangely set and shrined in circumstance.

Ah! did the brook sob hoarse, the dark tree pine   135
With all its branches, when first I missed him hence?
And found him not, whether my erring feet
Followed the waste flowers up the upland side,
Or dipped in grass, or scaled the Poet's Rock,
Or slid beneath the pines in Wells' woods: 140
Did Nature bid me mourn? or was it but
The restless beating in my own vague mind
That drove me on? I know not this; but he
Had passed away forever from the hills.
No more for him, 'mid fallen waves of grass,   145
Mower or harvest hand shall mop his brows
And look across the sunshine: nevermore
Gruff village cur, or even the patient yoke
That after them draw the furrow in the field,
Shall seem to watch those footsteps.
      Years have gone   150
And, but with me, his memory must be dead:
Yet oft I see a Figure in the fields,
And scarce less real than his personal self,
Which ever faded as the foot drew near:
I often see the figure in the fields,   155

128 *thought*   E   *dreamed*

And hear low verses wailing in the wind,
And I have mourned for him and for his grief;
Yet never heard his name, and never knew
Word of his history, or why he came
Into this outskirt of the wilder land;   160
And know not now, whether among the roofs
He parted fair, or, as the people say,
Went off between two days, and left the woods
And wilds to mourn him, with the sighing stream.

The School Girl: an Idyll

The wind that all the day had scarcely clashed
The cornstalks in the sun, as the sun sank,
Came rolling up the valley like a wave,
Broke in the beech, and washed among the pine,
And ebbed in silence; but at the welcome sound,   5
Leaving my lazy book without a mark—
In hopes to lose among the blowing fern
The dregs of a headache brought from yesternight,
And stepping lightly lest the children learn,
I from a side door slipped, and crossed a lane   10
With bitter Mayweed lined, and over a field
Snapping with grasshoppers, until I came
Down where an interrupted brook held way
Among the alders. There, on a strutting branch,
Leaving my straw, I sat and wooed the west   15
With breast and palms outspread as to a fire.
The breeze had faded, and the day had died:
And twilight, rosy-dark, had ceased to climb
Above the borders; when through the alder thicks

156 *wailing* ORIG:*sighing*   160 *outskirt* ORIG:*section*   164 *wilds*
ORIG:*vallies*   *with the sighing stream* ORIG:*ere the winter come*

9 *learn,* E *hear*

A school girl fair came up against the brook   20
From dell and gurgling hollow, where she had stopped
To pull sweet flag: and she had been below
Where the brook doubles,—for well I knew each knot,
Angle, and alnage of the weedy stream,—
For those pale amber bellworts wet with shade: 25
A girl, whom the girl mother's desperate love
Had clung to, through the years when, one on one,
All of her blood had blushed to drop away;
And she was left the last, with this one tie
To hang her to the earth: so young her life,   30
Above the gulf, detached, and yet detained,
Suspended swung: as o'er a fresh-fallen pool
A laurel-blossom, loosened by the rain,
Hangs at its pistil thread, hangs, shakes, and falls.

I saw her crossing through the alder thicks   35
And flowerless spoonwood: but, when she stopped to speak,
I seemed to lift my head out of a dream
To gaze upon her, for the ceaseless chime
Of insect voices singing in the grass,
Ticking and thrilling in the seeded grass,   40
Had sent me dreaming. I mused, and consciously,
In a half-darkness, so would sink away:
But ever and again the soft wind rose,
And from my eyelids blew the skimming sleep.
I looked upon her and her eyes were wet,   45
While something of her mother's color burned
Gay in her cheek: too like her mother there,
She stood and called me from the land of dreams.

The land of visions: but she, lingering, seemed
Most like a vision, standing in her tears,   50
Speaking unreal words: but when I sought
Their import, she said again in clearer tone
Her salutation, and asked did I not fear

51 *sought* ORIG:*asked*

The night's unwholesome dew? and offered flowers.
And as we wandered homeward by the slopes,   55
And through the sugar-orchard to the hill,
She told me of her griefs:—her music lesson—
She could not play the notes, nor count aright:
And she had sung before she broke her fast
That morning, and needs must weep before she slept; 60
And so throughout the day: until at night,
As she was winding upward by the brook,
The thought of her dead mother crossed her heart,
And with it came the fear that she herself
Would die too, young.   I spoke some soothing words, 65
For her frank sorrow yielding sympathy;
And as we rose the hill, stood for a breath,
And told an Indian story of the place,—
Of Wassahoale and the fair Quaker maid,
Who left the log-hut for a chieftain's lodge,   70
Until her face grew clear again and calm,
Yet like a sky that cleareth in the night,
Presaging rain to follow: we wandered on
But ere we reached the village she said farewell,
Nearing the house in which her father dwelt: 75
Her father, and his brother, and herself.
But I passed on until she left me there
At her own garden gate, with a half-smile
And eyelashes fresh-pointed with her tears.

Two brothers were they, dwelling in this place   80
When first I knew their names and history,
And held for heirs upon the village street;
Yet trained to work from starlight until dusk
For their old father: but he now was old,
Reputed rich, and like the bark to the tree: 85
Tougher perhaps, but tight enough for that.

69-70: These lines, not contained in MS, follow the text of E. See line 124
and footnote.   73 on E down;   77 passed MS past   84 father MS Father

And so they toiled and waited, stretched and scrimped,
With one maid sister fitted to reserve,
Early and late, until their hands were hard
And their youth left them. Still the promised day   90
Drew nearer,—the day of rest and competence;
And years went round, and still they rose and slept,
Not for themselves, but him who harder held,
Like a man drowning, his remorseless gripe
As his strength went. At length, when hope was o'er,   95
The very doorstones at the door worn-out,
And they themselves grown old, the old man died
And left them poor at last, with a great house
That fed upon their substance like a moth.
Bond debt and meadow mortgage had the rest—   100
All but the house—a sorry patrimony:
Today I saw it, staring, lacking paint,
With a new suit of shingles to the sky,
Spruce-pine perhaps, but sapwood at the best,
Good for five years, and warranted to rot.   105

Regardless this; but she of whom I spoke,
The elder brother's child, was like a light
In the blank house: not practical in truth,
Nor like the father's side, as oftentimes
The child is more the mother's than the man's,   110
But dearer far for this: and in the porch,
Where, for a mortal lifetime certainly,
Was seen the old man sitting like a stone,
Gathered young footsteps, and light laughter ran,
And sweet girl-voices. Once indeed I saw   115
An awkward youth in the dark angle there,
Dangling and flapping like a maple key
Hung in a cobweb; but she still was kind,
Gentle with all, and, as she seemed for me
Beside the brook, thoughtful beyond her years.   120

104 *Spruce-pine*   ORIG:*Chestnut*   105 *five*   E *three*

That night I scarcely slept before I dreamed
Of softly stepping in the meadow grass
With moccason on foot: and like, indeed,
The Indian of the story that I told;
While she who wandered with me in the day,   125
Still went beside; yet changing in her turn,
Became the truant daughter of the woods!
Now seemed herself, now Phoebe Bellflower,
And neither now,—but on I passed alone.
And like myself, thro' dewless bent and reed,   130
Brooding again the school girl's simple griefs,
And her sweet farewell face, and murmuring soft
These words:

    Sleep, sister, let thy faint head fall,
      Weary with day's long-fading beam,   135
    And blessed Gloom, in interval
      Of daylight, bind thine eyes and seem
    To lead thee on through darkling dells,
      Trembling with tiny harps and bells.
    The flowers you found along the day,   140
      While balmy stars of midnight shine,
    May those forgetting fingers sway:
      And so, until the morning stream,
    May all of fair and good be thine,—
      Gathered from daylight, or dim hours   145
    When balmy stars of midnight shine.

    Rest, maiden, let thy sorrows rest:
      Nor tearful on the future look,
    The sinless secrets of thy breast—
      And close the record like a book.   150
    And thus aside forever lay
      The disappointments of the day:

124: *the story that I told*. This is a reference to lines 69-70; like them,
lines 123-130 do not appear in MS. I follow the text of E on the presumption
that Tuckerman directed the printer to interpolate.
  135 *beam*, E *gleam*; 138 *darkling* E *dim-lit*

Nor note nor number bid thee weep;
 But lie, lie on, and let thy dream
Dim off to slumber dark and deep: 155
 I heard the whisper of the brook,
While the dry fields across the stream,
 With myriad-music of the night,
Still shook and jingled in my dream.

A SAMPLE OF COFFEE BEANS

Twelve plain brown beans! 'Twould seem to ask
 As plain, indeed, a string of verses:
Yet beans are sweet; but still my task
 Must tell of these, and, what far worse is,
A story dry for centre-block   5
 Whereon to shape fair Truth, or shun her;
Yet might I garnish up the stock,
 And hang it with a scarlet runner.

The bean, the garden bean, I sing,
 Lima, mazagan, late and early,   10
Bush, butter, black eye, pole and string,
 Esculent, annual, planted yearly:
Sure here a poet well might fare,
 Nor vaguely his invention worry;
I shake my head in flat despair;   15
 Or out and over the hills I hurry,
As Io fled by Nigris' stream,
 Spurred by the angry brize or bot-bee:

The full title: *A Sample of Coffee Beans, Sent to the Author with a Re-
quest for a Poem; or, The Publican, the Peddler, and the Poet*   3 Yet ᴇ
But *but still* ᴇ *and though*   4 *tell of* ᴇ *deal with*   5 *for centre-block*
ᴇ *must dress or dock*   6 *Whereon to shape* ᴇ *So to search out*   7 *might*
ᴇ *may*

Yet beans I sing, a classic theme
　　Known to the Muse; and may they not be　　　　20
Melodious made in other than
　　The lyric verse or amoebaean,—
Beans, hateful to the banished man,
　　And banned by the Pythagorean?

Loose, or in legume blue and red,　　　　　　　　25
　　Tinged like a tom-turkey's wattle,
Or strung like birds' eggs on a thread,
　　Or stiff and dry in pods they rattle;
Beans too, in bladders, discomposed
　　By stroke and blow, make music mystic,　　　30
But these are free in hand, nor closed
　　In their own natural cells, or cystic.
May I not, inly pondering, see,
　　Or stumbling on in flight phrenetic,
Enough of truth and simile　　　　　　　　　　35
　　To strew the way with flowers poetic?
No! though on every side they fell,
　　Dispersed like the gold hemony
On Ulai's bank, with asphodel,
　　Lote, lily-blow, and anemone,　　　　　　　　40

Beans would be beans, the gardener's joy;
　　And though to him more dear than roses,
Not to be made to senses coy
　　Rose-redolent, by any process
Let me then cease to stir my breast,　　　　　　45
　　No longer stay to bribe or flatter
The vegetable text: but rest,
　　Or get at once into my matter.

A little public-house and bar,
　　Barn, corn-house, dovecote, gathered under　　50
A mighty elm, which, arching far,

19 *Yet*　ᴇ *But*

[127]

Held off the rain and drew the thunder:
A farmstead small of shabby huts,
　　Unknown to cane or cotton grower,
And just within the line that cuts　　　　　　　55
　　The States and Canada the Lower:

A little public-house and bar
　　Smelling of beer and dead tobacco,
It stood: within, a bench and chair,
　　A parrot and an ape; but Jacko　　　　　　60
Was stuffed above the chimney-piece,
　　And Poll was plaster; so we summon
The holders of our house of ease,
　　And live incumbents, man and woman.

Jolly and old the landlord was,　　　　　　　65
　　Part farmer and part broadcloth-smuggler;
The wife a patient drudge, alas,
　　With aches and asthma long a struggler.
Yet day and night she served the grate:
　　He scarcely passed beyond the groundsill;　　70
But, feet in slipper-shoes, sat late,
　　And drew his ale, and kept his counsel.
Above his head an almanac
　　Depended, while the slate and pencil,
On toddy stick and tumbler rack,　　　　　　75
　　Kept watch and stood to charge or cancel:
Nought else except a faded, grim,
　　Fly-spattered print of Buonaparte,
And the host's Sunday hat and trim
　　Hung, like their owner, plump and hearty.　　80

Another too, a poet slim,
　　Came nightly from the neighbor village
To this retreat: more sweet to him
　　Than leafy summer house or treillage

70 *passed* MS *past*

Wherethrough the moonbeams fall. The wreath   85
    Trailed from the pipe of passing drover,
More rare than the grape blossom's breath
    Or nightgusts o'er the beds of clover.

In the world drama he was one
    Bearing perhaps a part like Peto   90
In the old play, yet did he shun
    The world, and, reckless of mosquito
By pondhole dark, and weedy drain,
    Sequestered swamp, or grassy sidehill,
Would linger, breathing dull disdain   95
    In many a rustic ode and idyll;

And breathing beauty too, and wit:
    Nor lacked it in poetic ardor,
His verse, for where he doubted it
    He struck again and hammered harder: 100
'Twas hit or miss, to make or maul,
    Not quite a Walter Scott or Byron,—
Two blows upon the anvil fall,
    And one upon the burning iron.

Good fellow was he in the main.   105
    Yet strangely strove to be unhappy,
Himself a desert chief would feign,
    And Cowcliff, Ararat or Api:
Or all alone would weep to cleanse
    Some fancied shame or felony;   110
Or, witchlike, haunt the birchwood glens
    For vervain dank and chelone.

A chamber, too, he had at times
    For needful rest; but his ambition
Was still to read and rant his rhymes,   115
    Unwearied with their repetition;
Or over some old tale bemused
    To lie, till chilled and hunger bitten,

Along a floor with books confused
    And blotted sheets, and reams unwritten.   120

Full well he knew the stars and flowers,
    The atmosphere, its height and pressure,
The laws that gird the globe, and powers
    That make our peril or our pleasure.
He knew each bird, its range and sphere;   125
    For plant and shrub, had many an odd use:
But naught of farming-growths or gear,
    And less of garden-sauce and produce:

So when the peddler passed, and brought
    His last new lot of lies and lumber,   130
Tins, foot-stove, gridiron, pail and pot,
    And drugs and dry-goods without number;
Segars too, in the grocery line;
    Tracts, extracts, jellies, quince or guava,
And rarest, seed for coffee vine,   135
    Pure bean or berry, just from Java;

He listened: "Sure to sprout: in fall
    To ripen, let the world go onward,
A row of oaken scrags was all
    They needed, so to scramble sunward."   140
"O happy thou," the schoolslip read,
    "Who with thy hands thy fortune carvest,"
But happiest, so the peddler said,
    Is he who gets such grain in harvest.

And so they talked: the summer wind   145
    Came softly from the meadow blowing,
Through open door and window-blind
    Brought the pine's breath across the mowing:

120 *reams unwritten*   ORIG:*rolls o'erwritten*

[130]

It stirred the print, it jarred the slate,
    It waved the farmer's best apparel,   150
And shook the dry weeds in the grate,
    And withered grasses, awn and aril.

And still they talked; and ere the wind
    Had faded, all that parcel precious
Was to our hero's hand resigned   155
    For future use: may such refresh us,
And him who held his luck revealed:
    His own, no doubtful risk or far gain,
But silver planted, sure to yield,
    And bless him with a golden bargain.   160

And then the landlord drew his best;
    No hoarded drops of vintage fruity,
But good to speed the parting guest
    And cheer the new: so while in duty
The poet drank, and called for more,   165
    The landlord, like a desert sandy,
The peddler parted, richer for
    Six dollars and a slug of brandy.

What more? Why naught: 'twere slow to tell
    The sequel here; such Glaucian traffic   170
May well befit a Homer's shell
    Or Virgil's harp; or, sung in Sapphic,
Perhaps 'twould mount a theme divine;
    But in this mess of jar and jingle
'Twould pose the nine brains of the Nine   175
    To make much sense and music mingle.

Yet might I tell how hard he wrought,
    Rising betimes to watch his purchase,
And left his rhymes and dreams forgot,
    And lonely walks beneath the birches;   180
And how the vines got riper fast,
    Till, battered pan with saucepan clinking,

[131]

He borrowed fire, and saw at last
   His prize, burnt, ground, and hot for drinking;

And how the Poet stirred and supt   185
   With an old spoon new-bought at auction,
And thought the world's ways all corrupt,
   For so he found his pure decoction:
Not fragrant, black, and fit indeed
   To set before a King or Sophy,   190
But slatestones for his silver seed!
   And for his coffee-bean, bean coffee!

His letter, too,—'tis here, addressed
   To some society Botanic,
In languid ink; though fitted best   195
   On wharf and mart to scatter panic.
A massive missive certainly,
   Nor writ with rifled plume or seraph;
See here, the dotless *j* and *i*
   Deform, with sprawly date and paraph.   200

And last, not least, could I repeat
   The landlord's glee, when, thither poking,
The poet sneaked into his seat,
   And all the glory of the joking:
How the old fellow roared, forsooth,   205
   And laughed from shining poll to shoelap,
Whilst the old lady showed her tooth
   And coughed, and shook the double dewlap.

Enough! the house still stands the same,
   With barn and steadings; but the elmtree   210
Went down in a great blow that came
   To flatten fence and overwhelm tree:
Yet looks the ale-bench on the way,
   And, as of old, the twain divide it;
But since the coffee-trade, they say,   215
   The peddler has not passed beside it.

183 *borrowed fire* ORIG: *gathered tools* 190 *Sophy*, E *Sophi*;

A LATTER-DAY SAINT

A gray old man, with a descending beard
Rugged and hoar, and a still massive face,
Met daily in the way: mall, market place,
Byway, and thoroughfare his steps have heard
At night and noon: the voice, the utterance slow,   5
And downward gesture like a blacksmith's blow,
Regardless ear, and eye that would not see,
Or saw as if it saw collectively,—
Who does not call to mind? We thought of all,
Resembling him to each one,—Plato, Paul,   10
Or him who round besieged Jerusalem
Fled, shrieking woe!—woe to himself and them,
Until the catapult dashed out his life:
Here, on this slab, above the tear and strife.
He stood and saw the great world fume and foam on,   15
As on a dial-plate, himself the gnomon;
Or, like old Time, he leaned on his scythe-snath,
Waiting the harvest of the day of wrath,
Now reaping-ripe: anon, with word and blow,
He thunders judgment to the throngs below: 20
The end of things he prophesies and paints,
And of the rest remaining for God's saints;
To one conclusion all his reasons run,
And this he sees, taking his hearers on
From point to point, though still discursively   25
The addle-eggs about his temples fly.
Again he wanders on, you wonder where,
And follow pityingly, but miss him there;
Forgetful soon, you join the stream and stress
Of the great Street; when to yon Porch superb,   30
Behold, the crowd runs, blackening flag and curb,

12 *Fled* ORIG:*Ran* 27 *on,* E *by—* 31 *Behold,* E *Behold!* MS
Behold

[133]

As to their Stoa the Athenians ran,
Or Rome to hear her Statius: you rush on;
And, in the middle of the jeering press,
He, smeared with mud and yellow yolks is,   35
Giving the law, like Zeno or Zamolxis.

ANYBODY'S CRITIC

Keen, brilliant, shallow, with a ready phrase
To fit occasion, and a happy knack
Of adaptation where he most did lack,
And witty too, and wise in several ways;
As knowing where to choose, and where to skip: 5
"Passwords of inspiration" on his lip,
He takes the wall, and now may well surprise
Those who remember him five lustrums back,
A ferret-headed boy with purry eyes.
Behold the Scholar now, the Judge profound!   10
Yet, feeling with his foot precarious ground,
He stands to fly, or with a borrowed jest
To blink the question when too closely pressed:
Reproof in praise, and friendship in his frown,
Have we not seen him, talking calmly down   15
On some proud spirit; letting light illapse
On him, poor votary of the book and pen?
Every way his superior, perhaps
A mighty poet before common men
Ashamed: but view our critic, mark his eye   20
Exhaustive, nose would snuff the violet dry
Of odour, and a brow to whelm the world.
In his right hand a written leaf is twirled.
Before, a landscape spreads, and there you see,
Skirting the sky, low scrub and topping tree.   25

1 *Keen* ORIG:*Cold*   13 *pressed* MS *prest*

[134]

Beside him stands a youth with bended eyes,
Waiting the word until the Master rise,
With blushing brow, less confident than cowed:
Perhaps his poem in his hand he brought;
Or a late letter from some lord of thought, 30
Like a rich gem, half-grudgingly he shows;
Of which a young man might full well be proud;
So cordial, sweet, and friendly to the close,
With not one vacant word of cant or chaff.
"Yes, yes," the Master says, "an autograph! 35
And surely to be prized, for such things *sell*:
And, for your poem, 'tis a clever thing."
Then turning the poor pages carelessly,
As taking in the whole with half an eye,
He said, "The worth of such 'tis hard to tell: 40
If Art inspire us, 'tis in vain we sing,
If love of Nature merely, 'tis not well,
And personal themes have little good or harm;
For in these bustling days, when critics swarm,
No man can stand aside without rebuke 45
To prate of bubbling brooks and uplands grassy;
Like the Pied Piper in the Burgelostrasse,
'Twill set the rats a-running." Then with a look,
A look that took the beauty from the grass
And dulled the blue, he let the subject pass 50
For other themes; glancing at, Heaven knows what,
The farm, the camp, the forum, Pitt and Burke;
And in his confidential, friendly phrase
Touched that, he knew the other valued not
Or plainly lacked, and of his life's best work 55
Spoke easily, with depreciating praise.

---

40 *'tis hard to* ORIG:*we scarce can*   50 *dulled* E *damped*   51 *glancing at,* ORIG:*discussing*   54 *Touched* E *Weighed*   55 *plainly lacked* ORIG: *did not have*

Rhotruda

In the golden reign of Charlemaign the king,
The three and thirtieth year, or thereabout,
Young Eginardus, bred about the court,
(Left mother-naked at a postern door),
Had thence by slow degrees ascended up: 5
First page, then pensioner, lastly the king's knight
And secretary; but held these steps for naught
Save as they led him to the Princess' feet,
Eldest and loveliest of the regal three:
Most gracious too, and liable to love.   10
For Bertha was betrothed, and she, the third,
Giselia, would not look upon a man.
So, bending his whole heart unto this end,
He watched and waited, trusting to stir to fire
The indolent interest in those large eyes,   15
And feel the languid hands beat in his own,
Ere the new spring; and well he played his part,
Slipping no chance to bribe or brush aside
All that would stand between him and the light,
Making fast foes in sooth, but feeble friends.   20
But what cared he, who had read of ladies' love,
And how young Launcelot gained his Guinivere,
A foundling too, or of uncertain strain?
And when one morning, coming from the bath,
He crossed the Princess on the palace stair,   25
And kissed her there in her sweet disarray,
Nor met the death he dreamed of in her eyes,
He knew himself a hero of old romance,
Not seconding, but surpassing what had been.

7 *but*   ᴇ *yet*   22 *Guinivere,*   ᴇ *Guenovere;*

[136]

And so they loved, if that tumultuous pain   30
Be love,—disquietude of deep delight,
And sharpest sadness: nor though he knew her heart
His very own,—gained on the instant too,
And like a waterfall that at one leap
Plunges from pines to palms, shattered at once   35
To wreaths of mist and broken spray-bows bright,—
He loved not less, nor wearied of her smile;
Yet through the daytime held aloof and strange
His walk, mingling with knightly mirth and game,
Solicitous but to avoid alone   40
Aught that might make against him in her mind;
Yet strong in this, that, let the world have end,
He had pledged his own, and held Rhotruda's troth.

But Love, who had led these lovers thus along,
Played them a trick one windy night and cold: 45
For Eginardus, as his wont had been,
Crossing the quadrangle, and under dark,
No faint moonshine, nor sign of any star,
Seeking the Princess' door, such welcome found,
The knight forgot his prudence in his love;   50
For lying at her feet, her hands in his,
And telling tales of knightship and emprise,
And ringing war; while up the smooth white arm
His fingers slid insatiable of touch,
The night grew old: yet of the hero-deeds   55
That he had seen he spoke, and bitter blows
Where all the land seemed driven into dust
Beneath fair Pavia's wall, where Loup beat down
The Langobard, and Charlemaign laid on,
Cleaving horse and rider;—then, for dusty drought   60
Of the fierce tale, he drew her lips to his,
And silence locked the lovers fast and long,
Till the great bell crashed One into their dream.

The castle-bell! and Eginard not away!
With tremulous haste she led him to the door,   65
When, lo! the courtyard white with fallen snow,
While clear the night hung over it with stars.
A dozen steps, scarce that, to his own door:
A dozen steps? a gulf impassable!
What to be done? Their secret must not lie   70
Bare to the sneering eye with the first light;
She could not have his footsteps at her door!
Discovery and destruction were at hand:
And, with the thought they kissed, and kissed again;
When suddenly the lady, bending, drew   75
Her lover towards her half-unwillingly,
And on her shoulders fairly took him there,
Who held his breath to lighten all his weight,—
And lightly carried him the courtyard's length
To his own door; then, like a frightened hare,   80
Fled back in her own tracks unto her bower,
To pant awhile, and rest that all was safe.

But Charlemaign the king, who had risen by night
To look upon memorials, or at ease
To read and sign an ordinance of the realm,—   85
The Cunigosteura or Fanolehen
For tithing corn, so to confirm the same
And stamp it with the pommel of his sword,—
Hearing their voices in the court below,
Looked from his window and beheld the pair.   90

Angry the king, yet laughing half to view
The strangeness and vagary of the feat:
Laughing indeed! with twenty minds to call
From his inner bed chamber the Forty forth,
Who watched all night beside their monarch's bed   95
With naked swords and torches in their hands,
And test this lover's-knot with steel and fire;

86 *Cunigosteura or Fanolehen*   E *Fanolehen, or Cunigosteura*

[138]

But with a thought,—tomorrow yet will serve
To greet these mummers,—softly the window closed,
And so went back to his corn-tax again.   100

But with the morn the king a meeting called
Of all his lords, courtiers and kindred too,
And squire and dame, in the great Audience Hall
Gathered, where sat the king, with the high crown
Upon his brow, beneath a drapery   105
That fell around him like a cataract!
With flecks of color crossed and cancellate;
And over this, like trees about a stream,
Rich carven-work, heavy with wreath and rose,
Palm and palmirah, fruit and frondage, hung.   110

And more the high Hall held of rare and strange,
For on the king's right hand Leoena bowed
In cloudlike marble, and beside her crouched
The tongueless lioness: on the other side,
And poising this, the second Sappho stood,—   115
Young Erexcea, with her head discrowned,
The anadema on the horn of her lyre;
And by the walls there hung in sequence long,
Merlin himself, and Uterpendragon,
With all their mighty deeds, down to the day   120
When all the world seemed lost in wreck and rout,
A wrath of crashing steeds and men; and, in
The broken battle, fighting hopelessly,
King Arthur with the ten wounds on his head.
But not to gaze on these, appeared the peers.   125
Stern looked the king, and, when the court was met,
The lady and her lover in the midst,—
Spoke to his lords, demanding them of this:
What merits he, the servant of the king,
Forgetful of his place, his trust, his oath,   130
Who, for his own bad end, to hide his fault,
Makes use of her, a Princess of the realm,
As of a mule? a beast of burden! borne

[139]

Upon her shoulders through the winter's night
And wind and snow? "Death!" said the angry lords;   135
And knight and squire and minion murmured, "Death!"
Not one discordant voice: but Charlemaign,
Though to his foes a circulating sword,
Yet, as a king, mild, gracious, exorable,
Blest in his children too, with but one born   140
To vex his flesh like an ingrowing nail,
Looked kindly on the trembling pair, and said:
"Yes, Eginardus, well hast thou deserved
Death for this thing, for, hadst thou loved her so,
Thou shouldst have sought her Father's will in this,— 145
Protector and disposer of his child,—
And asked her hand of him, her lord and thine.
Thy life is forfeit here, but take it, thou!
Take even two lives for this forfeit one;
And thy fair portress,—wed her; honor God,   150
Love one another, and obey the king."

Thus far the legend; but of Rhotrude's smile,
Or of the lords' applause, as truly they
Would have applauded their first judgment too,
We nothing learn: yet still the story lives,   155
Shines like a light across those dark old days,
Wonderful glimpse of woman's wit and love,
And worthy to be chronicled with hers
Who to her lover dear threw down her hair,
When all the garden glanced with angry blades!   160
Or like a picture framed in battle-pikes
And bristling swords, it hangs before our view:—
The palace court white with the fallen snow,
The good king leaning out into the night,
And Rhotrude bearing Eginard on her back.   165

CORALIE

Pale water flowers
That quiver in the quick turn of the brook,
   And thou, dim nook,—
Dimmer in twilight,—call again to me
Visions of life and glory that were ours   5
When first she led me here, young Coralie.

No longer blest:
Yet standing here in silence, may not we
   Fancy or feign
That little flowers do fall about thy rest   10
In silver mist and tender-dropping rain,
And that thy world is peace, loved Coralie?

Our friendships flee—
And, darkening all things with her mighty shade,
   Comes Misery: 15
No longer look the faces that we see
With the old eyes, and Woe itself shall fade,
Nor even this be left us, Coralie!

Feelings and fears,
That once were ours, have perished in the mould,   20
   And grief is cold:
Hearts may be dead to grief, and if our tears
Are failing or forgetful, there will be
Mourners about thy bed, lost Coralie.

The brook-flowers shine,   25
And a faint song the falling water has,
   But not for thee;

I follow the stanzaic pattern in MS; the E "Coralie" appears with the first
line of each stanza indented.

[141]

The dull night weepeth, and the sorrowing pine
Drops his dead hair upon thy young grave grass,
My Coralie! my Coralie!   30

———————

I took from its glass a flower
To lay on her grave with dull accusing tears;
But the heart of the flower fell out as I handled the rose,
And my heart is shattered, and soon will wither away.

I watch the changing shadows,   35
And the patch of windy sunshine upon the hill,
And the long blue woods; and a grief no tongue can tell
Breaks at my eyes in drops of bitter rain.

I hear her baby wagon,
And the little wheels go over my heart: 40
O when will the light of the darkened house return?
O when will she come who made the hills so fair?

I sit by the parlor window
When twilight darkens, and winds get cold without;
But the blessed feet no more come up the walk,   45
And my little girl and I cry softly together.

As Sometimes in a Grove

As sometimes in a grove at morning chime,
        To hit his humor,
The poet lies alone and trifles time,—
        A slow consumer:
While terebinthine tears the dark greens shed,   5
        Balsamic, grument,

44 *darkens*   E *deepens*

5 *greens*   ORIG: and E *trees*

[142]

And pinestraws fall into his breast, or spread
    A sere red strewment:

As come dark motions of the memory,
    Which no denial   10
Can wholly chase away; nor may we see,
    In faint espial,
The features of that doubt we brood upon
    With dull persistence,
As in broad noon our recollections run   15
    To pre-existence;

As when a man, lost on a prairie plain
    When day is fleeting,
Looks on the glory, and then turns again,
    His steps repeating,   20
And knows not if he draws his comrades nigher,
    Nor where their camp is,
Yet turns once more to view those walls of fire
    And chrysolampis:

So idleness, and phantasy, and fear,   25
    As with dim grandeur
The night comes crowned, seem his who wanders here
    In rhyme a ranger;
Seem his, who once has seen his morning go,
    Nor dreamed it mattered,   30
Mysterious Noon, and, when the night comes, lo,
    A life well-scattered

Is all behind, and howling wastes before:
    O that some warmer
Imagination might those deeps explore,   35
    And turn informer.
In the old track we paddle on, and way,
    Nor can forego it;
Or up behind that horseman of the day,
    A modern poet,   40

We mount, uncertain where we may arrive
　　Or what we trust to,
Unknowing where indeed our friend may drive
　　His Pegasus to:
Now reining daintily by stream and sward　　　　45
　　In managed canter,
Now plunging on, through brick and beam and board,
　　Like a Levanter!

Yet ever running on the earth his course,
　　And sometimes into,　　　　　　　　　　50
Chasing false fire, we fare from bad to worse;
　　With such a din too—
As this that now awakes your grief and ire,
　　Reader or rider
Of halting verse; till in the Muse's mire　　　　55
　　We sink beside her.

O in this day of light, must he then lie
　　In darkness Stygian,
Who for his friend may choose Philosophy,
　　Reason, Religion?　　　　　　　　　　　60
And find, though late, that creeds of good men prove
　　No form or fable,
But stand on God's broad justice, and his love
　　Unalterable?

Must he then fail because his youth went wide?　　65
　　O hard endeavor
To gather grain from the marred mountain side;
　　Or to dissever
The lip from its old draught: we tilt the cup,
　　And drug reflection,　　　　　　　　　　70
Or juggle with the soul, and so patch up
　　A peace or paction;

Would carry heaven with half our sins on board
　　Or blending thickly

Earth's grosser sweet with that, to our reward   75
    Would mount up quickly;
Ready to find, when this had dimmed and shrunk,
    A more divine land,
And lightly, as a sailor climbs a trunk
    In some dark pineland.   80

Truly a treasure in a hollow tree
    Is golden honey,
Breathing of mountain dew, clean fragrancy,
    And uplands sunny;
But who, amid a thousand men or youth,   85
    Landward or seabred,
Would choose his honey bitter in the mouth
    With bark and beebread?

No! though the wish to join that harping choir
    May oft assail us,   90
We scarce shall find vague doubt, or half desire
    Will aught avail us;
Nor fullest trust that firmest faith can get,
    Dark fear supplanting;
There may be blue and better blue, and yet   95
    Our part be wanting.

Alas! the bosom sin that haunts the breast
    We pet and pension;
Or let the foolish deed still co-exist
    With fair intention.   100
From some temptation, where we did not dare,
    We turn regretful;
And so the devil finds his empty snare?
    Not by a netful!

O conscience, coward conscience! teasing so   105
    Priest, lawyer, statist,

94 *Dark* ᴇ *Cold*   103 *And so the devil finds his empty snare?* ᴇ *Yet*
think "the Devil finds his empty snare,"

[145]

Thou art a cheat, and may be likened to
    Least things or greatest:
A rocking stone poised on a lonely tower
    In pastures hilly,   110
Or like an anther of that garden-flower,
    The tiger-lily,

Stirred at a breath, or stern to break and check
    All winds of heaven;
While toward some devil's dance we crane the neck 115
    And sigh unshriven;
Or lightly follow where our leaders go
    With pipe and tambour,
Chafing our follies till they fragrant grow,
    And like rubbed amber.   120

Yet, for these things, not godlike seems the creed
    To crush the creature,
Nor Christly sure; but shows it like indeed
    A pulpit preacher,
To fling a pebble in a pond and roar   125
    "There! sink or swim, stone,
Get safe to land with all your ballast, or
    Black fire and brimstone!"

Ah, in a world with joy and sorrow torn,
    No life is sweeter   130
Than his, just starting in his journey's morn;
    And seems it bitter
To give up all things for the pilgrim's staff
    And garment scanty;
The moonlight walk, the dream, the dance, the laugh, 135
    And fair Rhodanthe.

And must it be, when but to him, in truth,
    Whom it concerneth,
The spirit speaks? Yet to the tender tooth
    The tongue still turneth.   140

110 *pastures* ORIG:*uplands*

[146]

And he, who proudly walks through life, and hears
    Paean and plaudit,
Looks ever to the end with doubts and fears,
    And that last audit.

But, as we sometimes see before the dawn,   145
    With motion gentle,
Across the lifeless landscape softly drawn
    A misty mantle:
Up from the river to the bluffs away,
    The low land blurring,   150
All dim and still, and in the broken gray
    Some faint stars stirring:

So, when the shadow falls across our eyes,
    And interveneth
A veil 'twixt us and all we know and prize;   155
    Then, in the zenith,
May heaven's lone lights not pass in wreaths obscure,
    But still sojourning
Amid the cloud, appoint us to the pure
    And perfect morning.   160

And even here,—when stretching wide our hands,
    Longing and leaning
To find, 'mid jarring claims and fierce demands,
    Our strength and meaning:
Though troubled to its depths the spirit heaves,   165
    Though dim despairing,—
Shall we not find Life's mesh of wreck and leaves
    Pale pearls insnaring?

Yes,—as the waters cast upon the land
    Loose dulse and laver,   170
And where the sea beats in, befringe the sand
    With wild sea-slaver,—

163 *claims* E *aims*   167 *Shall* E *May*

[147]

For currents lift the laden and the light,
    Groundswell and breaker;
Not weedy trash alone, but corallite,   175
    Jasper, and nacre.

And though at times the tempter sacks our souls,
    And fiends usurp us,
Let us still press for right, as ocean rolls,
    Wtih power and purpose,   180
Returning still, though backward flung and foiled,
    To higher station,
So to work out, distained and sorely soiled,
    Our own salvation.

Nor following Folly's lamp, nor Learning's lore,   185
    But, humbly falling
Before our Father and our Friend, implore
    Our gift and calling:
Outside the vineyard we have wandered long
    In storm and winter;   190
O guide the grasping hands, the footsteps wrong,
    And bid us enter

Ere the day draw to dark: nor heave and prize
    With strength unable,
Nor range a world for wisdom's fruit that lies   195
    On our own table.
So shall we find each movement an advance,
    Each hour momentous,
If but in our own place and circumstance,
    Thou, God, content us.   200

Mark Atherton

Of one who went to do deliberate wrong,
Not driven by want, nor hard necessity,
Nor seemingly impelled by hidden hands
As some have said, nor hounded on by hate,
Imperious anger, nor the lust of gold,   5
This story tells. Yet all of these colleagued
To drive him at the last, who in young life,
Ere the bone hardens, or the blood grows cold,
When youth is prompt to change, even momently,
With every whiff of wind or word of chance;—   10
Through heat and cold for many a month and day
Went calmly to his purpose with still feet;
No breakneck speed, but fearfully, and as one
Who holds his horse together down a hill.

Bethiah, or, as those who loved her loved   15
To call her, Bertha, for her beauty's sake,—
Bethiah Westbrooke was a forest-flower
That trembled forth on the waste woods and swamps
Of wild New England, in the wild dark days
Of witchcraft, and of Indian wiles and war.   20
Yet something after this; for oft at night,
When Westbrooke's cottage was a beacon star
To many a beating heart, and suitors came
From far with gifts and game, then the old man
Who felt the fire, and had a gust to talk,   25
Would tell of Philip's war and Sassacus;
And how De Rouville crossed the crusted snow
Towards doomed Deerfield in the winter's morn,
With a quick rush and halt alternately,

28 *Towards* E *Toward*

As 'twere the empty rushing of the wind,   30
So to delude the outposts; how by night,
About the lonely blockhouse and the mount,
The scouting Indian hovered like a wolf,
Seeking a crevice to thrust in the fire;
Till the dumb creatures of the barn and field   35
Would give swift notice of the stealing foe;
Cows, horses, snuffed the warpaint, and, in the house,
How the dog whimpered with erected hair,
And, like the wind in a window, wawled the cat.
Of these and personal scapes would Westbrooke speak 40
As of the past: "For now," he said, "the tribes,
Shot, scalped, and scattered, flee on every side;
Their bark-boats staved and sunk, their lodges burned,
And plantings, and even the lands that grew them, seized;
They scarce can draw to head: the Indian war   45
Was ended, save that, perhaps, in the long nights,
From some lone farm outlying, a fire might rise,
Set on by the wild savage with a shriek!
For squads were here and there, and still 'twas said
That in the North some stragglers held together;   50
But mainly broken now; nor seemed it best
To mull and grind them into very dust."

And then the old man, turning as he talked
Towards his daughter, bitterly would speak
Of that most hateful sin of treachery: 55
False friendliness, and that domestic treason
Wherein the red man, trustless, merciless,
Is better than the white; then, pausing long,
Would gaze upon Bethiah where she sat,
Till the girl winced, and on her forehead stood   60
The impatient color; and Mark, Mark Atherton,
Into his dark avoiding eye would seem
To call a clear look, till the old man's fell.
Not lovers these, though long-accounted friends;
And, though the voice went that they two would wed, 65
Not lovers sure; yet the youth had her ear

And ready laughter, for he well could speak
Smooth words, but with an edge of meaning in them,
Like a sharp acid sheathed in milk or oil.
Others too held aloof, but still the maid   70
Heard not, or, hearing, heard with a half-heart;
For still another stood between the two,—
Companion of the twilights and the dawns
Of parted days, one who had loved her then
With true-intending love,—his hope, his star,   75
And almost mistress; and so the maiden looked
On this and this, with a divided eye.

Into the forest rode Mark Atherton.
Leaving the settlement at the river-side,
By felling and burnt-over land he passed, and plunged 80
Through towering fern and thickset, till he reached
The open pines; and onward still he rode,
Climbing the slippery slope, and clattering down
The stony hollow: from his horse's hoof
The shy frog flew, and, like a streak of light,   85
The squirrel darted up the mossy bole,
Where, glancing upward, downward, and across,
Hammered and hung the crested popinjay.

So sharply on he rode; now brooding on
His purpose, which was in truth to win the maid, 90
Wrong her rich love, and sell her to the chiefs
That lurked with their red warriors in the shade;
Now on her beauty with a grain of ruth,
Their long-time friendship, and that marriage vow
Which his heart hated: for he thought of one,   95
Once the heart's idol of his boyish dream,
That hardly heaven seemed fitted to enshrine;
Now pent within a house just bigger than
A martin-box, that seemed, and scarce as clean:—
The fair slight girl that was,—and see her now!   100

70 *still*   E *yet*   80 *passed*   MS *past*

A dozen children at her gowntail pull,
As so a slut as ere went down at heel!

So, hardening his heart, he drew his rein
Against the bank, and sought the waterside;
Parting the laurel to behold thy face,   105
New England's stream, dark River of the Pines!
There lay and listened till the twilight fell;
When, weary of the flutter of the leaf,
The dipping of the ripple on the rock,
And plaintive calling of the phoebe-bird,   110
He chanted, half in fear, half-mockingly:—

"The river sides are high, the night is dark,
And fair white hands are drawing at our bark;
Tonight, tonight, the winds obey our call,
And the still dark river sucks like a waterfall,   115
As downstream in the dugout on we fare;
For the minister's daughter and deacon's wife are there,
        Paddle away!

On either bank, as softly down she plies,
Remember, remember, that many a landing lies: 120
Then fear not the Friend with whom we have our part;
Nor shame to own the love that hideth in the heart;
Nor grudge our chiefest chamber to afford,
When the house is his from sill to saddle-board;
        Paddle away!"   125

                And with the cadence came
The quick replying plunge of a broad blade;
And, hideous in his paint and peag, with face
Inflexible of mournful gravity,
An Indian chieftain, leaping from his boat,   130

106 *dark*   E *cold*
112: E reads
        "The river-sides are high, are high, the night is dark!
119: E reads
        On either bank, as softly, softly down she plies,

Stood like the fiend evoked. But Atherton,
Whose cheek had whitened like the winter leaf
That flickers all day in the whistling beech,
Held down his head as for a moment, so
Recovering his face; then steadfastly   135
Exchanged due greeting with the forest king,
And passed they into parley by the stream.

Red light had parted from the westward verge,
And night lay black, ere back again and fast
The horseman fled, a shadow through the shade.   140
And now indeed, as if in very truth,
The river-demons gathered on his track;
For, ever as he rode, a woman's shriek
Seemed to pursue him through the sounding pines!
And where he looked there was a woman's face,   145
With the frothed lip, and nostril edged with blood,
Relentlessly appealing, as it seemed;
And ever as he rode a ceaseless sound
Went ringing at his ear like jingling gold;
And, like the innumerable chink and chime   150
Of the night crickets hidden in the grass,
Not to be lost or left; he gnashed his teeth:
But even there the forest fell away,
And on, by burned and blackened stumps and shells
That mimicked all things horrible and vague   155
In the dim glimmer insecure, he sped,
And gained the pickets of the palisades.

Another night, and later in the year,
A youth and maid, in the first edge of dark,
Stood by the haunted stream, or wandered on,   160
Insensibly approaching in their talk
A bushy point that jutted from the wood:
Alley and ambuscade of black pitch pine.
Various their look: he, lowering in his mood,

137 *passed* MS *past* 157 *palisades* E *palisade*

[153]

Baffled and broken where his heart was high, 165
Strode sullenly; she, sad but resolute,
And pale with her determination, yet
As one who strives to soothe a cureless harm,
Spoke tenderly, as to an angry friend,
Remembering old affection ere he go. 170
"Partings must be," she said, "but is not this
A sorrowful leavetaking to our love?
To all our friendliness an ill farewell?"
A moment more, and while the words were warm,
Torn from her feet, arms bound, and gagged with grass, 175
They trailed her through the thickets of the wood.
And all alone stood Atherton with him,
The sachem of the riverside and stream,
Receiving now what he had had in part,
All the bad wage of his iniquity. 180
Then, as if all things now were at an end,
Released from gift of faith, and entergage,
They parted silent: one took up the trail,
The other slowly to the village passed,
And raised the alarm, and blew the gathering horn, 185
And headed the wild search.
                              With trampling feet
He led them to the River, where, he said,
They dragged her through the stream and up the bank,
He following on into its very flow;
But his foot slipping in the anchor-ice, 190
With wetted gun, and bruised among the stones,
He saw her, for whose life he risked his own,
Snatched from his sight; but darker now the night,
They far before, the trail unsure by day:
What more could be, but gather arms and men? 195
And scout abroad, and watch till morning light?

And Westbrooke, the old man without a child,
Now raging, now in blank and mute despair,

184 *passed* MS *past*

[154]

Ran forth, or stood in helplessness of grief:
Not now as when he marched with Mosely's men   200
Against the savage seated in his strength:
When, like a sword of fire, with twenty more,
He fell upon their necks and drove them in;
Or under Winslow, in that desperate day,
When, beaten off by the red foe intrenched,   205
Through battle smoke he found himself alone
O'er breastwork and abbatis charging back.
Gone was his strength, and, as the days went by,
Gone seemed his heart. He sought his bed, and there,
Seeing but one face as the days went by,   210
Lay motionless; and like a drowning man,
Who, lying at the bottom of a brook,
Stares at the sun till, small and smaller grown,
It flickers like a lamp and then goes out:
So shrank his hope, so dropped into the dark.   215

And days went by, and still no tidings were.
The smouldered war broke up in fresher flame,
Killing all hope; the rangers, ranging back
Through all the Massachusetts, west and north,
Had swept the woods to farthest Canada,   220
And many prisoners ransomed or retook:
But she, the glory of his life, was gone.
And yet, one winter morning, ere the sun
Had crossed the River on his westward march,
Sudden as was the stroke, the mercy came;   225
And Westbrooke held the daughter of his heart;
Wilted and wan, yet still the Forest-Flower!
Brought by the party of a friendly tribe,
Who took her from the chiefs, sick unto death,
And nursed her long, and tenderly led her home,   230
Nor claimed reward.
                    And sudden vengeance broke

202-203: Tuckerman interpolated these lines at some time between the
original composition and the printing; they are written after the end of the
poem in MS.   211 *Lay*   MS *Laid*

[155]

On him, the traitor; but not by those he had wronged:
Fled on the instant to the cedar swamps,
His Indian allies seized and bound him there;
And after battle, smarting for their slain,   235
There, in the darkness of the cedar swamp,
They slowly burned his flesh and charred his bones.

So, in the old days, God was over all,
Vengeance was full, and wrong returned to right;
Mercy replied to Love; the lost was found;   240
And treachery answered so with treachery.

SIDNEY

Have you forgotten that still afternoon?
How fair the fields were, and the brooks how full?
The hills how happy in their hanging green?
The fields were green; and here, in spots and holes
Where the rich rain had settled, greener green.   5
We sat beside a window to the south,
Talking of nothing, or in silence sat,
Till, weary of the summer-darkened room,
I in an impulse spoke, you smiled; and so
In this consent we wandered forth together   10
Across the fields to entertain the time.

Shall I retrace those steps until we reach
Again the crossing River? Yes; for so
Again I seem to tread those paths with you:
Here are the garden-beds, the shrubbery,   15
And moody murmur of the poising bee;
And here the hedge that to the River runs.
Beside me still you moved through meadow flowers;

235 *smarting* ORIG:*chafing*

[156]

Beside, yet unapproached; cold as a star
On the morning's purple brink; and seemingly   20
Unconscious of the world beneath your feet.
Yet as I plucked up handfuls from the grass,
With here and there a flower, telling their names
And talking ignorant words of why they were,
You paused to gather berries in the hedge;   25
And I despaired to reach you with my words,
Believed you cold, nor wished to find myself
Calling your face back, and as in a dream
Lingering about the places where you were;
And would not if I might, or so it seemed,   30
Attain unto the property of your love:
Knowing full well that I must soon awake,
Gaze blankly round, and, with a bottomless sigh,
Relapse into my life;—the life I knew
Before I saw your fair hair softly put   35
From off your temples, and the parted mouth,—
More beautiful indeed than any flower,
Half-open and expectant of the rain.
O youth and loveliness! are ye less dear
Placed at impracticable height, or where   40
Not wholly clear, but touched with shades and spots
Of coldness and caprice? or do such make
The bright more bright, as sometimes we may see
In the old pictures? Is the knight's brow held
Not noble for its scar? or she less fair,   45
The lady with the lozenge on her lip?
So may your very failings grace you more;
And I, most foolish in my wisdom, find
The grapes alone are sour we cannot gain.
But, Sidney, look! the River runs below,—   50
Dark-channelled Deerfield, here beneath our feet,
Unfordable, a natural bar and stay:
Yet, ere you turn, let us look off together,
As travellers from a hill; not separate yet,

25 *in* E *from*

[157]

But being to be divided, let us look   55
Upon the mountains and the summer sky;
The meadow with the herd in its green heart;
The ripple, and the rye grass on the bank,
As what we ne'er may so behold again.
And do me right in this; the eye that saw   60
These accidents and adjuncts could not fail
To mark you, loveliest of the place and time;
A separate beauty, which was yet akin
To all soft graces of the earth and sky,
While wanting naught that human warmth could give. 65
So, lady, take the bitter from my words:
Let us go onward now; and should you prize
In any way the homage of a heart
Most desolate of love, that finds in all
Still the salt taste of tears, receive it here,   70
With aught that I can give, or you retain.
Let me, though turning backward with dim eyes,
Recover from the past one golden look,
Remembering this valley of the stream,
And the sweet presence that gave light on all,   75
And my injustice, and indeed your scorn,
Refusing me the half-stripped clover stalk
Your fingers picked to pieces as we walked.
Yet, ere we part, take from my lips this wish,—
Not from my lips alone, from my heart's midst,—   80
That your young life may be undimmed with storms,
Nor the wind beat, nor wild rain lash it out,
But over change and sorrow rise and ride,
Leading o'er all a tranquil, lenient light;
And, when your evening comes, around that beam   85
No tragic twilight brood, but late and long
May your fair beauty linger like a star,—
Like a pure poignant star in the fleecy pink.

72 *turning*   ORIG:*looking*   87 *May your fair*   E *Your crystal*

But give your poet now one perfect flower,
For here we reach again the garden's bound,   90
Sweet as yourself, and of one lustre too;
Yet not the red dark bud Damascus yields,
Nor York and Lancaster, nor white, nor yellow
But a rose-colored rose.

REFRIGERIUM

Let them lie,—their day is over;
   Nought but night and stillness be:
Let the slow rain come and bring
   Brake and stargrass, speedwell, harebell,
All the fulness of the spring;   5
   What reck I of friend and lover?
Foe by foe laid lovingly?

What are mounds of green earth, either?
   What to me unfriendly bones
Death hath pacified and won   10
   To a reconciled patience,
Though their very graves have run
   In the blending earth together,
And the spider links the stones?

To the hills I wander, crying,   15
   Where we stood in days of old,
Stood and saw the sunset die;
   Watched through tears the passing purple,—
O my darling! misery
   Has been mine; but thou wert lying   20
In a slumber sweet and cold.

92: This line is not in MS.   93 *Nor*   MS *Not*
2 *Nought but*   E *Only*

THE OLD BEGGAR

When buttercups break on each grassy side,
And the summer-long clover is far and wide,
And by air-hung crag and gully dwell
The rasberry rose and the blue bluebell,
    What will he do? what can he say?   5
Will the lavish laurel his charges pay?
No; but the sun lies warm on the way;
And if today will not, tomorrow may!

Yet late in the year, when the grass is dry,
And the grain is all in, and the garden by,   10
And on reach of river, and forest through,
The smoke of the Autumn is brooding blue,
    What will he do? what can he say
To the purple swamp, and the hills' array?
Naught, but to whisper the adage gay,   15
If today will not, tomorrow may!

But now, when the white drift is hurrying higher,
And the birch log sputters like fat in the fire,
And the wind whistles boldly, and in the window
The weather-glass bubble is buried in snow,   20
    What will he do? what can he say?
Out! is it ours to save or to slay?
E'en let him go whistle his lesson and lay,
That, if today will not, tomorrow may!

Heed not his cry, though you feed of the best,   25
And with warmest of feathers have fledged your nest;
From the wind of his garments shrink and scowl;

19 *whistles* E *singeth*

Slap the door in his face, and let him howl!
    What will he do? what can he say?
What matter to us if we preach and pray?   30
Stand him aside for a fairer day!
So, if today will not, tomorrow may!

Alas! when the daylight is weary to see,
When the grasshopper's song shall a burthen be,
When the jar of the cricket is bitter to hear,   35
And the hum of the harvest fly stings the ear,
    What shall we do? what can we say
When the heart is old and the head is gray,
And Grief cometh home like a child to stay,
Nor if today will not, tomorrow may.   40

When we plant with tears, and in sorrow pluck,
And cometh cross-fortune and evil luck;
And the land is cold, and the stiff hands bleed,
And for harvest we hardly get back the seed,
    What can we do? what shall we say   45
If a selfish past we alone survey?
Dare we hope from the present a happier ray?
Or that, if today will not, tomorrow may?

Ah, no! but now reach him the holding hand;
Round his fading strength be an arm and band;   50
Be the wrong of the wretched your trust and task;
And when trouble comes home, then do you ask,
    What can we do? what shall we say?
Thank God for the good we have done in our day;
(Be the beggar's burthen our stave and stay,)   55
That the cloud may be lifted, with full heart pray,
And that, if today will not, tomorrow may!

40: In E the line reads
    And to-day cannot help us, nor morrow may?
57 *And that, if* E *And, if*

PAULO TO FRANCESCA

When weary Summer had laid down her leaves,
And all the autumn fields were brown and bleak,
How often did we, wandering cheek to cheek,
Tread these deserted ways: on those sad eves,

You—clinging to my side how fearfully!—   5
Would scarcely dare to speak or breathe aloud;
While every gust seemed like a voice to rise,
And Nature's self to mourn; how often we,
Low in the westward, where they stood like eyes,
Saw the Gemelli under brows of cloud!   10
Or, through dim pineboughs,—now the quick tears start,—
Watched the red beating of the Scorpion's heart,
While winged with love and fear the hours fled by.
O stolen hours of danger and delight!
O lamp of erring passion burned to waste!   15
O true false heart! even now I seem to taste
The bitter of the kisses that you gave.
You were the traitor,—yes; and more than I,
You were the tempter. Ah! that autumn night,
The hour that seemed a wavering line to mark   20
'Twixt early sunset and determined dark,
Found us together: menacing and grave,
The night sank down; no lingering gleam allowed,
But in the west one fiery cupreous cloud!
Do you remember, desperate in my mood   25
Of all things, of myself, and most of you,
Half careless too, whether the worst were known,
So that the storm might split on me alone,
I laughed to think how far we had gone from good?

29 *gone*   E *got*

Then, with a quick revulsion, wept to view   30
The misery of our lives, for cruel hands
Had digged a gulf between, a gulf of sin
We could not cross, nor dared to plunge within:
And yet, as musing on our fate and fall,
I spoke as one who surely understands,   35
Of that deep peace that had been found by some,
And good from evil; reasoning like Paul
Of temperance, judgment, and the life to come;
Deeming it better here to weep and fast
Than mourn with those who shall mourn at the last: 40
And we had wept as ne'er till then before,
And half resolved that we would meet no more;—
In the brush hollow, under the bare skies,
While darker yet the Shadow closed and clung,
You, pausing, turned—do you remember this?—   45
With clinging arms and die-away sweet eyes,
And kissed me in the mouth with such a kiss
As that Apollo gave Cassandra young,
Sealing her prophet lips, alas, with serpent tongue.

When the Dim Day

When the dim day is buried
    Beyond the world's sight,
Low-lingering, lurid,
    A sorrowful light
Is left on the hilltops;   5
    While bitter winds blow,

36: MS does not contain the word *had*.   43 *brush hollow*   E *pine-hollow*
48: *Cassandra*. Curiously, this is the only mythological reference which
bears a footnote in MS. Tuckerman wrote: "This young lady Cassandra
Young, [sic] was you know kissed by Apollo in the manner described, who
thereby falsified (to the ears of all hearers) & rendered null his gift of
prophecy."

Swept down from those chill tops
  And summits of snow.
Yet, like a pale crown set,
  The hills wear away   10
The gold of the downset
  And dying of day;
So the Indian beheld it
  Above his dark pine,
Ere the pioneer felled it: 15
  Yet, brother of mine,
No more by the River
  You track to the brink
Snowy marks of the beaver:
  The muskrat and mink   20
Are all that is left now;
  So nations depart;
And Nature, bereft now,
  Place yieldeth to Art.

Yes, bridgepier and building   25
  Now burden the bank,
Where the slow sunset, yielding,
  O'er dark forests sank.
Nor the red man with cunning
  His net hangeth here   30
Where the rapid is running,
  Nor plungeth the spear.
Yet raftsman and wrecker
  Subsist by the stream;
Here find their exchequer: 35
  Nor empty, we deem,
Are the boats and the barges
  That softly drop down,
Bearing burthen and largess
  Of hillside and town.   40

But the heart no change knoweth:
    The stream shifts its side;
Wind cometh and goeth,
    But sorrows abide:
The bank breaketh inward;   45
    The hills heave and sink;
Without and withinward
    All gather or shrink.
See where by yon birches
    The wave rested still;   50
Now the wild water lurches
    And lashes at will:
Nor oarsman nor sculler
    Could draw on the tide,
Though his cheek wore the color   55
    Of roses in pride.
But the depth and the deadness
    Of grief will not flow:
O sorrow and sadness,
    That this should be so!   60
Though the wave and the earthquake
    May swallow the shore,
Yet wild sorrow and heart-break
    Will part nevermore!

HYMN TO THE VIRGIN

Tu, O Virgo virginum,
    Flos et maris stella!
Lumen gestans hominum,
    Puritatis cella!
Maria, fons veniae,   5
    Fons mellis et roris,
Fons misericordiae,
    Pincerna dulcoris;

Porta regis gloriae,
 Omni pulchritudine   10
Siderum ornata:
 In polorum culmine
Regnas coronata.

TRANSLATION

Thou, O Virgin of the virgins,
 Star and flower of the sea!
Bearing up the Lamp of men,—
 Shrine of purity!
Mary, fountain of remission,   5
 Fountain sweet of honey-dew,
Fountain of forgiving mercy;
 Mingler and dispenser too
Of delightful sweetness;
 Gate of splendor's king,   10
In all excellence of beauty
 Stars out-glorying!
At the summit of the poles,
 Crowned, thou art reigning.

MARGITES

I neither plough the field, nor sow,
 Nor hold the spade, nor drive the cart,
Nor spread the heap, nor hill nor hoe,
 To keep the barren land in heart.

And tide and term, and full and change,   5
 Find me at one with ridge and plain;

And labor's round, and sorrow's range,
    Press lightly, like regardless rain.

Pleasure and peril, want and waste,
    Knock at the door with equal stress,   10
And flit beyond; nor aught I taste
    Disrelishing of bitterness.

And tide and term, and full and change,
    Crown me no cup with flowers above;
Nor reck I of embraces strange,   15
    Nor honey-month of lawful love.

The seasons pass upon the mould
    With counter-change of cloud and clear,
Occasion sure of heat and cold,
    And all the usage of the year.   20

But, leaning from my window, chief
    I mark the Autumn's mellow signs,—
The frosty air, the yellow leaf,
    The ladder leaning on the vines.

The maple from his brood of boughs   25
    Puts northward out a reddening limb;
The mist draws faintly round the house,
    And all the headland heights are dim:

And yet it is the same, as when
    I looked across the chestnut woods,   30
And saw the barren landscape then
    O'er the red bunch of lilac-buds;

And all things seem the same: 'tis one,
    To lie in sleep, or toil as they
Who rise beforetime with the sun,   35
    And so keep footstep with their day;

For aimless oaf, and wiser fool,
    Work to one end by differing deeds;—
The weeds rot in the standing pool;
    The water stagnates in the weeds: 40

And all by waste or warfare falls,
    Has gone to wreck, or crumbling goes,
Since Nero planned his golden walls,
    Or the Cham Cublai built his house.

But naught I reck of change and fray,   45
    Watching the clouds at morning driven,
The still declension of the day;
    And, when the moon is just in heaven,

I walk, unknowing where or why;
    Or idly lie beneath the pine,   50
And bite the dry-brown threads, and lie
    And think a life well lost is mine.

THE UNPUBLISHED POEMS

*

ODE: FOR THE GREENFIELD SOLDIERS MONUMENT

This slender spire of glossy stone,
   A nation's emblem poised above,
Speaks it to bleeding hearts alone?
   Ensign of sorrow and of love?

Or here, upon this village green,   5
   In half-light of the autumn day,
Meet we to mourn for what has been,
   A tale, a triumph passed away?

Yes, more: our gift is generous
   As theirs who gave their lifeblood free;   10
Not to the dead alone, to us
   Ourselves, and ours that yet shall be

We consecrate for distant years—
   No idle rite, our deep hearts stirred,
And tenderly, with prayers and tears—   15
   The gleaming shaft! the Eagle bird!

UNDER THE LOCUST BLOSSOMS

Under the locust blossoms
That hung and smelt like grapes:
Under the honey-locust blossoms,—
Faintly their breath escapes
And smites my heart; though years have passed since I   5
Beheld those clusters swinging silently,
Silver racemes against that sunset sky:

[171]

A sky all over rosy.
I waited for the night
Till the crickets tinkled drowsy   10
In their beds of clover white
Or fell silent at my footfall, one by one.
Did I wait? Did I wander there alone,
Under shadow, in that garden not my own?

'Tis but a shade of odour,   15
A recollected breath,
And I stand, a dark intruder
The swaying flowers beneath,
Alone, and peering on through anxious gloom
For a motion, for a glimmer; did it come?   20
Oh that moment! Oh that breath of locust bloom!

Lines Written in the Blue Ridge, Virginia

A man, an Irish man, 'tis true,
Came from his island hither,
Before the later autumn blew
And woods had left to wither,
To breathe an edge of mountain air,   5
A smack of mountain danger,
And gather fortune, friends, and fare:
A poet and a stranger

Come of that good old stock of old
Who deemed the world suspended   10
To minister to monks, and rolled
But as their fortunes tended;
Who saved their souls and spent their means,
Knew but one path to heaven,

21 *moment*   ORIG: *hour*

But well good brawn from pulse and greens   15
And always char from cheven.

He doubted, thought the world was well
Nor needed priests' redressing,
So left behind the sacring bell
Nor stood for ban or blessing;   20
He left behind the sacring bell
And "flat meads thatched with stover,"
Sought out a half-manned caravel
And worked his passage over.

Consistent! let us test his claims;   25
In wealth not worth a dollar,
Only the best now suits his aims:
A churchman and a scholar.
With buxom ale his heart he glads,
Drinks wine instead of water,   30
Nor cares for Little Iliads
Or Lady day the latter.

Vain, versatile, and fickle, lo!
To each strange pipe he dances,
Now crazed for newest glory, now   35
Half-mad with old romances;
Now goes unwashed and sinks his tone
To what his toil or trade is,
Now strolls a fop, his time his own,
And a mere man of ladies: 40

And May dew for a morning face
He thinks more rare confection
Than paints and pargets in their place,
Patches, pots of complexion.
Now half a boy he steals alone   45
And slow, through sun and shadow,
Looking for gold, the lapwing's stone,
Or mandrake, or right maddow.

And so time went: philosophy
He tried, then claimed invention   50
Of some new stop in poesy
With matters not to mention.
Too genuine far to make his mark
Mid tricksters and trepanners,
He lectures turned, and theses dark,   55
Fate, doctrine, men and manners

Most learnedly would talk upon;
And yet as one who jostles
The doers and the deeds in one,
Epistles and apostles: 60
O'er Scriptural names of Achsah, Ruth,
And Leah, would hitch and hirple
To Lydia, faithful to the truth,
A seller too of purple.

Nicaula, in her robes of state,   65
Dorcas, Demetrias, Lilias,
And men of might, the scarce known great
From Gilpin back to Gillias:
Strange peers in evil look and life,
Crooked Richard and Constandel,   70
He knew, and heads with learning rife
In Cork and Coromandel.

Yet never heeding place or kind,
Whate'er he gave his views on,
He all the wealth of all his mind   75
O'erturned in rich confusion;
Nor parted up his ware in lots
That all might portion fairly,
But proffered pearls and peridots
For better beans and barley: 80

And so they rent him, story old,
Till he cried, sick with striving,

[174]

"Pinchbeck and orsidue are gold!
And Fame is had for diving!"
Yet finding where one came to ground,   85
The water sure would drown ten,
He left the Mart and left the Sound
For breezes of the mountain.

He left the Mart and left the Strand,
And now our plot commences   90
To heighten, like the barren land
Beyond the fields and fences.
But more astray and ill at ease
We get, the higher clamber we.
"The morning is dark and smells of cheese"   95
Quoth Giles with his head in the ambery.

Keep courage! we shall see the light
And breathe the northwind blowing;
The little hamlet is in sight
Towards which our steps are going   100
Where, hidden in a mountain notch
Like gray bats clung together,
A quiet folk, and chiefly Scotch,
Had huddled from the weather.

A little Paradise it seemed,   105
Half-shadowed and half-whitened.
The slow cloud sailed, the sunshine gleamed,
The river dusked and brightened:
A little Paradise it seemed,
Worth losing name and fame for,   110
But ah! they cared not what he dreamed
But only what he came for!

Some said he was a landless lord,
And some a rogue of station,
And every movement, deed, or word   115
Lacked not interpretation.

[175]

And if he nothing did but sleep
Or shift his daily clothing,
"'Twas plain," they said, "he'd never keep
So calm a sough for nothing!"   120

And thus from hand to hand he flew;
Through tradesmen, herdsmen, mowers
Sped ball-like till he fell into
The Circle of the Sewers
Who weekly strive for charity   125
And heads to heap abuse on,
Whose lightest touch's profanity,
Whose handling is pollution:

Who fairest fabrics smirch and soil
Without one pleading voice,   130
Who never heard of Pope and Boyle,
And never read Pomfret's Choice;
Sisters of the consistory
Who make the village histories:
Some said it was a mystery,   135
Some said it was a mistress.

Poor devils! on their praise or ban
He little built or reckoned,
But fled as if from death he ran
And went where Nature beckoned.   140
Better to lie the turf below
The water where the moss sips
Than knitting lace like sad Rousseau,
Make peace with country gossips.

And thus upon the hills we met   145
Like patriots sick of mobrule,
Or mercury-drops of varying weight,
Yet blending in one globule;
And there this record line by line
Of strife, ambition, folly,   150

He told to me. The rhymes are mine,
The matter his—his wholly.

"And now," he said, "the world is done
For me, no world redressor,
Yet here a man the world might shun   155
And live his own possessor:
Nor help nor hindrance would he find
In upper world or nether,
Though he should feed him with the wind
And clothe him with the weather;   160

Here might be found a concave good!
Or made by boring-blasting,
And if Religion was his mood,
How fair a place for fasting!
Or would he pet his carnal sins   165
Nor take himself to task for;
Wild honey hoards and chinguapins
Are all a man could ask for.

He should not care in wine to wet
His barken loaf or bannock,   170
While from this ridge of mountain yet
Runs out the Rappahannock;
Nor like the swain who gets no crop
Save where he sets or seeds it,
He should find shelter when to stop   175
And meat where'er he needs it.

So might the poet cease to roam
Far shores and islands many
For fairer food than grows at home:
But here in Alleghany,   180
Nipping the verdure here along
These mountain necks and passes,
Hang like a goat to browse among
Poor pines and Indian grasses;

[177]

For thou, O Nature, tuft and tree,   185
A war with want still warrest
To feed thy children grudgingly:
And so these walks of forest
A natural sustenance, bleak and rude,
To mountain sheep and kid owe,   190
Sheddings and shack of the wild wood,
Woodchuck and chuckwill's widow.

Glean by the moon: and eft and fly;
In shower and sunshine flourish.
And only He, the Master high,   195
Finds naught or naught to nourish;
And shall it be he may not do
Like these with reason greater?
Perhaps remake himself anew
And be his own creator?   200

His spirit and his fleshly force
Corroborate so fully,
He should outrun the swiftest horse
And talk with angels duly;
With senses fined, with vision cleansed   205
From sin and self indulgence,
What light would be to him dispensed!
What glory! what effulgence!"

He ceased. A little wind rose free;
Far off we heard it humming.   210
"And like that wind," he said, "shall be
My going and my coming.
Here will I build, here fix my bridge
From here to the hereafter."
And fierce old Fell and Grummet Ridge   215
Shook softly as with laughter.

Too long a tale! We wandered down
To meet not on the morrow,

For he was gone, yet left for one
Some words of love and sorrow.   220
The little hamlet in the cleft,
Bequeathed his discontent to,
But ah! they cared not what he left
But only where he went to.

But this they never knew or found: 225
Perhaps across the ocean
He fled again to greener ground,
Found peace if not promotion.
Or if within these hills he stayed
In rest and golden quiet,   230
I wondered how his bed he made
And how he liked his diet;

And after, when the hills fell bare
And all the grass went reddish,
How fared he with his mountain fare: 235
Fall-feed and winter eddish?
And did he thus his days prolong?
And was his heaven the nearer?
And whether, while his legs grew strong,
He felt his head get clearer.   240

I wondered too if peak and wood
United to outbrave him,
Or took him to their brotherhood
With welcome wild and gave him
The freedom of their rocks and earth   245
And sky, for life a member—
And how he liked their mountain mirth
In snowtime and December.

I wondered then, I wonder now,
When gazing at the Grummet,   250

229 *stayed*   MS *staid*

[179]

Whether alone and gathering snow
He sits upon some summit,
Stylites-like, the storm to mock!
Or packed for Cork his seatrunk;
Or humbler namesake Simon Stock   255
Is living in a treetrunk.

The Shore

Again from the woods to the shore,
To the edge of the world where the world is all behind,
    Like the limit of life and death,
Where the wind is an opiate balm, and the soul shall
        remember her griefs
With a dull content at last, and dream and dream.   5

The wind blows in from the shore
The fresh salt smell of the weed with the briny shells,
    And my heart tides to and fro
For here were the lips so loving, here the hands that
        pressed into mine
With a happiness like pain, for love, for love.   10

I see the hills of the shore
And, above them, a belt of the ocean, dark and still,
    And my eyes come full with tears,
For the white sandhills of the shore, and the shore
        and the high blue sea
Bring back my grief, but never my joy, my joy.   15

'Twas here we stayed by the shore
So late that the lights on the water began to move,
    The beacon to glare and go;

16 *stayed*   MS *staid*   18 *beacon*   MS *Beacon*

For we said that the day should be dear, come weal,
    come woe, come boot, come bale:
Oh, dear, forever and ever to us, to us.   20

Alone at night on the shore
I stand, while the stormy beacon flares and fades,
    And look for a lost delight;
But the rising ridge far out, and the shock of the
    landing billow,
And the bitter backward wash, is all, is all.   25

NATURE AND NECESSITY

"Where shall we sleep tonight?" The woods hang leavier
    And we have far to get.
Your ankle's sprained, my shoulder carries weight:
This gun which has for hours been growing heavier—
    No pad or epaulet—   5
Bears downward like a bar from Gaza's gate!

Where sleep? why here, where boughs shake down their loose hair.
    We'll take of sleep our fill
On amber breathing beds, red drifted spines,
Hillocks, and littered heaps, like matted moosehair.   10
    We'll lie in slumber chill
Or wake and brood till the great morning shines.

Nothing can harm thee here, nothing come near thee
    By want or wonder stirred—
Save drifting owl or weakeyed whippoorwill.   15
Sad Weekoalis! did the chieftain hear thee
    Afar, thou spirit bird,
And turn his footstep from thy haunted hill?

22 *beacon* MS *Beacon*

[181]

"But no!" you say, "this is no place for stopping!
    The house we left behind,   20
Where we could get no speech or aught command
May yet be gained. The night is dark and dropping,
    The paths are hard to find,—
Lost and belated woods on every hand!"

Well go! and yet, as you began with us,   25
    Better keep on, or pass
The night here. Take that girl too, for your test:
That little ragged girl who ran with us
    Begging and whining as
A partridge runs to guide you from her nest;   30

Now buffets at your feet, now falls she down
    Because her brood is hatched.
I think 'twould move a heart of stone to see,
A heart of adamant or chalcedon,
    How pitifully she   35
Wept with one eye, and with the other watched.

You saw his hutch beside the cherry tree
    And heard his drunken song,
Though at our coming, something chicked and cowed;
How could he speak or hear, in faith and verity?   40
    A mitten on his tongue,
In either ear a whizzing locust loud?

But here we've shelter without rant or rumpus,
    Though hard to leave, I fear,
For even by day you could not see the sun.   45
With hardly light left now to read your compass,
    'Twill soon be midnight here,
Though outside, yet the daylight is not done.

What then? We breathe and taste; none sweeter can
    Wild scents the woodwinds waft.   50
Even the little wanderer's gamy trail,

Infecting a whole countryside, seems better than
    Ill odors of drain and draught
Rising round human roofs ere rain prevail.

Yet I have felt—and you will wonder straightway   55
    Or laugh, such words to win—
How strange a charm in some lone house we find:
What tears seem in the grass about the gateway!
    What aching pathos in
The clothes hung forth to beat in tossing wind!   60

Yes, let us walk slow, favoring your ankle,
    And I will strive to tell
What I have heard of him, your wished-for host.
Pause not, nor let the recollection rankle;
    You have not had your will: 65
Much have you gained thereby and little lost.

When first he came into this section, hiring
    A hand to build and clear,
He brought his wife, a damsel little skilled,
Felled a small space, enough for winter firing,   70
    Made out that hut to rear,
And, spectre-harried, ceased to clear or build.

Yes, cleared for action: built too, rough stockading
    With slits to fire through;
Prepared to sell his life, and not for naught!   75
And though no offer came, kept still parading
    Ghosts, devils, marching too—
In fact the man with fear was just distraught.

"What at?" Why loneliness, or too much thinking.
    The spirits of the waste   80
Knocked nightly at his door: such things have been
And till he burned his fence and fell to drinking
    He scarce could touch or taste
But that a ghostly hand would pass between.

A chipping bird, a common catbird mewing,   85
    He heard with secret awe;
Was "feared for Indians" too, kept his eye skinned,
Put out his vestal pipe and held to chewing
    For fear the wake should draw
And smelt a brush-heap fire in every wind.   90

But nothing Indian came but Indian summer:
    Faint shadow, twilight moon,
And far blue vapors on the dreaming pine.
So he turned in by day and took a rummer,
    Believed the sun, the moon,   95
And wondered why the stars forgot to shine!

And now,—you're surely better of your lameness—
    In his dismantled fort
He drinks and raves, scouts Satan and his crew.
The wife? She died of want of talk and sameness,   100
    Nothing to see, in short,
And children miss not what they never knew.

Poor things indeed! I would my tale were merrier;
    Yet 'tis no tale, but just
Amidst, without beginning or yet end.   105
But when cold blows, and even those woods get drearier,
    How they may live, or must,
I dare not think: but warm you may depend—

Hung up like bats, those selfish self-supporters,
    Or trunk-enharbored bear;   110
Like flitch of bacon in a reeky flue,
Or spider housed in kitchen chimney quarters,
    Or cobweb in cow's ear,
Or all; the fancy needs not to be new

So it be warm! Though cold and covetous   115
    You scarce could wish to share
That darkling den, rank as woodpecker's hole

[184]

With five white eggs within; but rather buffet us—
　　Let luckless be aware!—
Straight through the storms of fate to reach our goal!　　120

G. D. W.

A little band of friends were we.
　　Together still by steep and stream
We wandered joyfully, and he
　　The leader of our faith and dream.

We broke the flower and bent the weed;　　5
　　The berries caught, the river quaffed,
And if the world went wild indeed,
　　Looked in each other's eyes and laughed.

'Twas his to slight the louder world,
　　But for the brave, the fit, the few,　　10
'Twas his to speak like torrents hurled;
　　'Twas mine to find their teachings true:

'Twas his to fathom Nature's hoards,
　　Her hidden deeps, her brightest sky;
And mine perhaps to tell in words　　15
　　The visions of his wider eye.

And now we linger, one by one,
　　So vainly by the autumn boughs,
Or idly sit to weep, alone,
　　In the dark places of the house;　　20

And yet beneath the altering leaf
　　We linger round his glorious trance,
And I remain to sing a grief
　　Beyond all rhyme or resonance.

The eulogy is for Tuckerman's friend, George D. Wells.

[185]

What fitter earth to lay apart   25
   Him whom we prized all price above?
Here are the hills that nursed his heart,
   And here the valleys of his love.

So well he knew each watery nook,
   Each greener cave, each grassier sod;   30
So bland and beautiful his look,
   We called our friend the River god.

Here, where his early footsteps led,
   Our friend, our hero, only ours,
Bury the fair victorious head!   35
   And bid Columbia storm in showers

Her angry tears! a vengeful flood!
   And claim her own with wail and shriek!
New England's best and brightest blood
   Is scattered through that fatal week!   40

But here we find no battle stain
   For drops of death or rainy grief,
The plaintive falling of the rain,
   The glimmer of the wet red leaf.

Hushed are the horns, the bugle's call,   45
   The harrowing trumpet's fierce despite,
The guns, the battering drums, and all
   The tumult of the burial rite.

His river rolls as still it rolled:
   No burdened murmur from its bed   50
Seems grieving for the heart of gold,
   Seems mourning o'er the graceful head;

Yet Nature heeds—the faith he taught
   Be ours, as in those earlier years,

And thoughts the offspring of his thought   55
   Shall lie around his grave in tears.

All gracious emblems guard his rest:
   Of inborn gifts, or cultured powers,
The natural oakleaves on his breast,
   The cross of silvery outland flowers.   60

The long grass weeps, the high tree shower
   His threads in mornings dim and damp,
And o'er him at the midnight hour
   Great Lyra like a funeral lamp!

So much, yet more; our eyes swim dim—   65
   So destitute in grief we live,
We cry "When we have given him,
   What is there we have left to give?"

We give a life, a light removed:
   Our idol whom our hearts have known,   70
The playmate whom the children loved,
   The brother, son, and friend in one.

We give the Patriot, Soldier, Chief!
   The grandest e'er these valleys trod—
O Father! with our noblest grief   75
   We give to Thee our River god!

GUNHILDA

Gunhilda, lady of my love and theme,
Sister of kings, and daughter of the Dane,
Was by her brother Hardicanute betrothed
To him of France, the monarch of his time:
Henry the First of France, Niger surnamed,   5

A prince not overwise, and in his mood
Weak, passionate, superfluous, and proud;
But fond of honor, loving justice too,
If holding hard by cruel law be just,
Whose aim in his tumultuous reign had been   10
To keep his kingdom; to beat back the Hun
When from their fastnesses across the Rhine
Hand over head they came; to dine and sup;
To gather in his rents and royalties;
To poise and punish, and, for service done,   15
Reward in kind: though knowing but in truth
To mete and part his purple with the sword
Right regally and like that king of men
Who dipped his pearls by helmetfuls at once,
And with a spear sounded his depth of gold.   20

Not such the Princess: nor fit mate for such
In temper or in years. But that was naught:
He was a king who wooed, or sought to woo.
But she, a votaress whose vow had been
To dedicate her beauty and her youth   25
To God alone; whose earliest hope had been
To build and to endow a house to God;—
Turned from these tidings with a cry for help,
Knowing the king and fearing what she knew.
A nature too, averse from violence,   30
Cloistered and cold and nurtured in the shade
And like the nunflower swerving from the sun.
What wonder then that the king's flaming love
Among the convent shadows broke in at once
On her secluded mind unwelcomely?   35
And, like a window opened in a wall
When comes the day to faded bloodshot eyes,
No faint irresolute light, but like a blow!

So, and like one doubteth of the morrow,
Knowing the present and the peaceful past,   40
Is happy and desires not any change,

[188]

Among the rocks about the twilight bay,
Or lost in driftless musings on the sands
Where her great father bade the surge retire,
Gunhilda stood. And while her thoughtful eyes   45
Watched the decaying color in the cloud,
Watched the wave curl and pour, the pebbled beach,
And water running over water white,
Her deep heart trembled and her fear grew great.

But forward went the hours; the day was fixed   50
And Henry crossed the sea to claim his bride.
Small respite gave the fiery king, and she
Walked to her fate upon a cloth of gold
That stretched so far she could not see the end—
Through arch and column vibrating with light,   55
And drops wherein the live light seemed to hang
Like sunshine in the dew, all gleams and gems!
For the high porch was gay with essonite,
With amianth and mossagate, motherpearl,
Asterias and rockrubies, whilst the floor   60
With sanders sweet and safflower reeked in dust.
With pomp of music and with clash of swords:
So they were wed, and great rejoicings rose.

Nor seemed their happy progress stayed at length
When they arrived the king's voluptuous court.   65
So deep the draughts of love he daily drank
Unsatisfied from her angelic eyes,
So grew the rapture in his own, the queen
Began to fear such sunshine could not last,
And so it proved. There came about a change.   70
Perhaps 'twas overlove, the bitterness
Of too sweet kisses, or mere mad caprice—
Like him of whom the cruel story tells
Who slew his wife because she was so fair:
Slew her as she was stooping unawares,   75

42 *Among*   v *Upon*   52 *king*   MS *kings*

[189]

Incensed at that white wonder of her neck!
Or that the king indeed in his dark heart,
Knowing his heart and hers, could not believe,
Unworthy as he was, such majesty,
Grace, goodness, piety divine, could be   80
For him, or if for him, for him alone.

So, when a whisper stirred about the court
The queen was false, disloyal to her vow,
To all but her it broke expectedly.
And though none knew whence came the charge, or whose   85
The arrow, all knew in whose bow 'twas shot:
The purport too not less significant,
For in that day and time with such a charge
To be confronted was to be condemned.
And men began to talk below their breath   90
Of Judgment and the Fiery Ordeal,
The convent and the stake. But while they talked
With mouth to ear, or slunk in groups together
And questioned low whether the queen would be
Called over the coals for this, or what would be,   95

The word went forth that by the king's command,
In his great mercy not assigning death—
The instant death—for the committed crime,
In ten days' space, and at the hour of noon,
The cause itself should be contested by   100
Arbitrament of battle in the field,
And combatants, arms and armor left at choice.
Wherefore let him, the proclamation said,
The champion of the accusation, cite
Him of the vindication, if such there be,   105
Into the lists upon that place and time,
Before the judges . . . and God save the Queen!

God save her! yes, for the succor seemed
Farther than Heaven's, farther than heaven from earth!

   106 *place*   v *day*

[190]

Alone, without a friend or friend of friend: 110
A stranger among strangers! Of her train
All had returned before or been sent back
But Mimecan, the little Englishman:
Too slight to be accounted when they went,
Too young to give suspicion in that kind   115
For which she was arraigned before the world,
Too weak to aid in this her last distress.
So the poor queen sat shelterless like one
Around whose head the storms accumulate
When through cloud-ranges of the upper air,   120
Through cloudy clefts and pinnacles to cloud
From peak to peak, from vault to archevault
The thunders boom, the lightnings branch and glare.

Nor Henry walked at ease in his high halls.
Infuriate with himself and with the world   125
Whose censure yet he feared, as weak men will,
Now cursed, now wept, half-anguished in his mind
For her he had reprieved to certain death,
And all diffused; wherefore, at times, the king
To stun his thought, the noises in his ears   130
Bade all his trumpets blow at once, or sate
Buried in wine and made the daylight dark;
Or in the beat and blaze of fiery lamps
Looked upon troops of girls in crimson dight;
Yet still through all, taste, touch, form, silence, sound,   135
Or darkness or fierce carnal color, felt
The wakening of the worm that cannot die.

Thus when the morn rose dark of that dread day
It brought relief to both: respite to one
Eternal and most final for her pain   140
Unless a miracle should come between.
So, at the time appointed and the place,
From all sides in a mighty concourse rushed

116 *arraigned* MS *arrang'd*

[191]

Like winds that beat about their central calm:
A calm of death, for in that centre sat   145
The king with all his court, and near them drawn,
The judges and the judged. Gunhilda there,
Clad in attesting white, her eyes unraised,
Alone and with a lily in her hand;
Once she looked up and quickly saw the whole,   150
The barbarous king, the headsman with his axe,
The faces massed and the despairing sky;
Then thought of England and her wedding day:
This was the ending of the cloth of gold.

But why prolong the measure of her woe?   155
The pathos of a grief inestimable?
At the first trumpet's challenge, into the lists
Strode the King's Champion, huge, iron helmed
In back and breast with long stript battle brand,
And paused disdainfully, for no one came,   160
Though once again the bitter trumpet wailed.
Vast was the wonder and the pity too
When from the farther end, not near the queen,
At the last trumpet's charge, came Mimecan
Dressed like a page and tripping like a girl;   165
His station took and, at the encountering word,
Drew forth his trinket blade. The giant grinned,
Lashed at him with his sword, and grinned again.
Then, and like one who sought upon the place
To stamp the boy's life out among the stones,   170
Or puff him with a scornful breath away,
Sank point and stood. Instantly Mimecan
Sprang in, within his guard, and backwardly,
Before the other could wheel round his weight,
Hock-strung and felled him with one little blow.   175

Wild was the roar that rose and shook the heaven
With cry on cry, none louder than the king's,
Who left his throne to take her to his heart;
Proffered himself with all indemnity

Of life and love, jewels and nameless wealth,   180
For justice had been done! But she at once
Turned from the worldly king herself away
With a few parting and proud words.

                              "I go
To God," she said, "and leave this cruel world,
This cruel scene of terror and of shame   185
By thee devised I hardly know for what.
If thou believed me innocent, 'twas ill;
If guilty, then am I no wife for thee.
Nor could you bar my steps from this intent,
Not though you placed your throne across my path!   190
Or poured about my feet, to block the way,
Bullions of gold, billets of ebony,
Great opals, balais rubies, peregrine pearls!
For Heaven is just and will not see the wrong.
Wherefore take heed, O king! lest God himself,   195
In whose hand lie the hearts and thoughts of kings,
Should from thy brow set off the royal crown,
That gold incirculation, and pass down
The Sceptre haft incrustated with gems!
I go, but leave my place; and may it be   200
More worthily filled; and thou, if not more just
To her who comes, at least more merciful."

So ends the story of my tale. But she
Has gone to take her part in other fields
With others who have lived: with Imogen,   205
Rhotrude, Giserida, and she who died,
The Moorish Andamana. Among the rest,
And halfway turned, as if to view once more
The world that she was leaving, stands the Queen!
Alone and with a lily in her hand: 210
Gunhilda, lady of my love and theme.
She stands with rich sad eyes and ambern hair.

LONG ISLAND

I

Long Island, yes! When first my vision swept
Thy far faint shores, with inlet and lagoon
And misty woodflats, where the senses swoon
As in that land where Christian sank and slept,
I thought of him; and then when in the rain   5
We reach'd the Inn: but when I heard them speak
Of Fire Place at hand, and Devil's Neck
And Good Ground, and Mount Sion far away
As it should be: I seem'd to tread again
The Pilgrims' steps and trace the Heavenly Way.   10
But there sat Happy Jack and dumb Rejoice,
And Ike the hostler with his squealing voice,
And an old man I called Legality,
Crafty and quaint the tale he told to me.

II

"Young Silas Long, a carrier through these woods   15
Drove home one night in not the best of moods;
Having just seen a drown'd man flung ashore
With a strange feather cap: and once before
When he was hauling seine in Southold Bay
About this time of year, a seaman's corse   20
Wash'd up: With such a cap and such a face
And it had brought misfortune on the place.
Pondering he drove, when lo across the way
He saw too late, that there a body lay;
Felt the wheels tilt but could not stop his horse: 25
Or not at once: then flinging with a slap
The old cloth cover down he call'd a cap,
Ran back, ten steps or more, and nothing found.

Yes! the dead pines and deerfoot on the ground:
And so return'd apace in five or six: 30
His cap was gone! and in its stead thrown down
The very loonskin the twice-drown'd had on,
With bits of seaweed sticking to the flix!
So Long rode home, of cap and sense bereft
But still can show the dead man's that was left,   35
And the webs crawl he says when the sea rolls."
Then he, having told his tale and said his say
By way of emphasis and corollary,
Spat a torpedo in the bed of coals.
"And what, what, what," squeal'd Ike "became of Long's?"   40
But the old man here rose and reach'd the tongs,
Laid fire to his pipe and phew'd away.

AN INCIDENT

'Twas in the country's darkest hour of fear,
Perplexity, and peril. Overawed,
The world hung breathlessly: at home and near
Were bitter foes, and bitterer friends abroad,
Nor hope there seemed beneath the hearse of heaven.   5
On such a day of doubt, and silently,
We walked apart, the Englishman and I
Through low flat wood that, as we rose, rose higher.
A man he was, expatriate and self-driven
Beyond the deep; adrift, he cared not whither,   10
Hating his land and also hating ours;
In many things lacking the gift to see
And rating all he loved not rogue or liar,
Either of both, perhaps, or both in either:

12 *gift* v *sense*

Loving not man but yet humanity,   15
Loving the white Truth as a boy his bride,
Loving the sun, the ground, the growth, the showers,
Believing too in God and destiny
And in the general uselessness of life.

"Behold," at length he spoke. "The brother strife   20
Is well nigh ending now, and what betide,
The country is no more, her flag is furled!
And can it be that these our foolish eyes
Shall see the close that almost saw the rise?
America! the country of the world!   25
The half-the-world that should have changed the whole,
The model flowering of all modern time,
Dropping to pieces like a three-days rose?
The rise we saw not, but we see the close:
But on the earth no promise of the prime,   30
Nor in the cloud of heaven from pole to pole!"

"Not so!" I said, "or if so, not so yet!
Our own is ours, and I must first forget,
Ere I forego one petal of my Flower,
All happy days and dreams of happy youth,   35
That Spring will come again, that winds will blow;
The early vehement hope, the faith unshaken,
The deep obliging vows our hearts have taken,
And once for all, to strike in danger's hour
And strive and overcome for Her and Truth!   40
And shall 1 droop because my Cause is low?
Blood of myself! not so! whilst thou canst flow
Or give one drop to victory's holy shower!
Still must I deem with him whose precepts say,

The darkest hour is just before the day: 45
And if the day be cloud, the land be dearth,
He looketh on with far foreshadowing eye,

38 *The*   v *With*   41 *shall*   v *must*

[196]

Sees in the fruitless earth more fruitful earth,
And in the sky, the sky beyond the sky!
And more and most, in war began the Slave;   50
In war must cease, his lifebirth and his grave.
Rolled as through blood, the Realm will reach repose;
Cooled as from fire, the clefted Land will close,
And battle's field, like a late up-ploughed lot,
Return to fresher growths where these are not.   55
Nor more to hear, our anguished hearts will beat
The midnight raid, the skirmish, the retreat:
All this shall pass—the smoke shall draft aside,
The kine shall low where late the cannon roared,
And in those vales where now the hurrying sword   60
With blood for sweat is reaping to the quick,
The farmer shall again his sickle put.
And where red Strife has stamped with angriest stride,
Mid its own orchard bowers again shall hide
The cottage home with its small children, like   65
The bird's nest set in the print of a horse's foot."

He smiled, but now a whisper far and sweet
That seemed to rise again and faint and flee
Came to us of the distant mountain breeze.
He smiled but answered not, and on we wound   70
Still through the woods until our weary feet
Still through the woods, but rising latterly,
Gained a high place at last above the trees,
A sere and desolate spot: on every bound
Dark woodsides pressing up, and more remote   75
On the land's edge, a single parted pinetree.
"Cans't thou then find," he said, "mid outskirts wintry
That golden grace of Spring? thine early creed?
Vows of observance which in youth thou sworest?
Ah, not as now we linger, caring not   80
That life has failed with us, half proud indeed

50 *more* v *last* 60 *vales* v *fields* 75 *woodsides* v *woodlands* 77
outskirts v *regions* 78 *thine early creed* v *those dreams of thine* 81
half proud indeed v *in truth half proud*

[197]

That we have striven, or loved, or suffered wrongly,
Firm in despair or faltering in contrition."
Beyond the mountain and the climbing forest,
Beyond the ribs of the far separate pine,   85
Suddenly struck on my averted vision
A single star through twilight twinkling strongly,
A single beam stirring its misty shroud:
Of a world's hope the visible flag and sign,
Beneath a single bloodbright stripe of cloud.   90

88-89: v omits.

APPENDIX I

*

THE EDITORIAL PROBLEM in Tuckerman involves an inquiry into the nature and authority of the texts through which the poems have come down to us and, in particular, an inquiry into the matter of punctuation. The published texts are few, and the manuscripts upon which they are based appear to be the only extant texts in Tuckerman's hand. The manuscripts, however, do not represent a fair copy of the poems as we may suppose the author finally intended them; their punctuation is generally inconsistent and frequently ill-chosen.

In the preparation of the present text, I have been influenced by one wish above others: that of preserving, as far as normal grammatical usage will allow, the poems that Tuckerman wrote. A considerable amount of intrusion has been necessary. Tuckerman was not a grammarian; he was inordinately fond of commas and colons, and he inserted them with a free hand. The editor of the 1860 edition of the *Poems*, in solving one problem, created another. He improved upon the quality of Tuckerman's punctuation, but his own text is over-punctuated. Subsequent printings of the *Poems* contained no revision of punctuation. Not until Bynner's edition were the sonnets allowed to flow with the sound which Tuckerman must have heard in his own mind. But Bynner's habits were too liberal. Not only did he do away with much of the punctuation; he "corrected" a significant part of the diction and syntax as well. In Sonnet IX of the third series, for example, the final line reads as follows in the manuscript:

Dim fades, and as the sun fades, fades alike, like dim.

Bynner altered the line to read

Dim fades and, as the sun fades, fading likewise dim.

To the extent that the line is less confused, Bynner's version is perhaps an improvement. But it strikes me that the ownership of the poem has changed hands in a small but important way. I have followed the manuscript in this instance because I can see no valid reason to do otherwise. Except in a very small number of cases, the kind of which I am about to illustrate, I have not altered the diction or syntax of the manuscripts. In Sonnet V, fourth series, however, I have followed Bynner's example. The eighth line of the poem in manuscript reads as follows:

If ill$_\wedge$ sneereth, yet abides the good.

Bynner changed the line to read

If evil sneereth, yet abides the good.

It seems to me that the alteration is justified for reasons of metrical improvement. Moreover, by inserting the caret, Tuckerman indicated that he was himself aware of the problem; it seems likely that he would have concurred in Bynner's choice. I have been careful to footnote variations other than those of punctuation, and I believe it possible, through the use of the footnotes, to reconstruct the substance of the manuscripts. Notwithstanding, I have had to be judicious in the use of footnotes. Were I to account for every revision of punctuation, the text might well seem subordinate, and the purpose of the edition would be frustrated.

The present editorial procedure, and the nature of the editorial problem in general, may best be described with reference to a particular, complete poem. The manuscript version of Sonnet IX, first series, is as follows:

Yet wear we on, the deep light disallowed
That lit our youth, in years no longer young

[200]

We wander silently, & brood among
                    break
Dead graves, & tease the sungleam & the cloud
For import: were it not better yet to fly,
                              throng
To follow those that go before the crowd
Reasoning
Stepping from stone to star & easily
Exampling this existence? or shall I
Who yield slow reverence where I cannot see
And gather gleams where'er by chance or choice
                          falteringly
My footsteps draw, though glimmeringly dispensed
Come into light at last? or suddenly
Struck to the knees like Saul, one arm against
The overbearing brightness, hear, a voice?

At the bottom of the manuscript page the words "falter," "fit-
ful," "broken," "duskily," and "waver" are written. Probably Tuckerman considered each of these words in the penultimate position
of the eleventh line. Both "glimmeringly" and "falteringly," Tuckerman's first and second choices in point of time, are metrically un-
suitable. The word "brokenly" seems to me (as it seemed to Bynner
and the editor of the 1860 edition) to be the best of the suggested
alternatives. The punctuation of the first sentence in general, and
the comma following the word "hear" in the final line, are ex-
tremely problematical.

The version which I have included in the present text retains
the diction of the manuscript version with one exception: "brokenly" in line eleven. I have worked on the assumption, of course,
that MS Am 1349 (2) is the final draft from which the 1860 edition of the *Poems* was produced. The present version of Sonnet
IX departs in fewer instances from the manuscript than does either
the 1860 or the Bynner version. In the second line I have placed a
semicolon where Tuckerman has a comma. The last half of the
first line and the first half of the second constitute a parenthetical
element which confuses the sentence as a whole. It appears to me
that the semicolon after the word "youth" in the second line better
enables the sentence to be read without confusion. The 1860 version attempts to surmount the difficulty by the use of a dash, and

Bynner saw fit to terminate the initial sentence at that point. In both cases—especially in that of the Bynner version—the caesura is given more weight than I can suppose Tuckerman intended. In the third line, Bynner, by omitting the comma after the word "silently," has disposed of a pause that should, I believe, be retained. The same is true of Bynner's omission of the comma in line four. In line five, both Bynner and the editor of the 1860 edition place a period where Tuckerman has a colon. It seems to me that the colon produces a caesura of considered quality, and I have retained it. In line six I have retained Tuckerman's word "that" where Bynner and the 1860 editor substituted the word "who." I have, that is, preferred to retain Tuckerman's usage rather than to change the word. In line nine the 1860 editor placed a comma after the final word. The natural pause at the end of the poetic line seems to me of sufficient length without the comma, and I have therefore followed Tuckerman's example. At the end of the eleventh line, however, the quality of the natural pause seems wanting, and I think it desirable to follow the lead of the previous editors. As did Bynner, I chose to omit the comma which Tuckerman seems quite arbitrarily to have placed after the word "hear" in the final line. In lines eight and twelve Tuckerman inserted question marks in the interior of sentences. I have capitalized the word "Or" in line eight because it can begin a complete sentence and because the capitalization requires no sacrifice of meaning or movement.

The chronological order in which the poems were written, and their dates, cannot be determined exactly. MS Am 1349 (2), which contains all of the poems printed in the 1860 edition, bears the date 1854. Some of the poems, if not all, were transcribed from an earlier source. The poem "May Flowers" was composed no later than 1850, the year in which it appeared in *Littell's Living Age*. "Picomegan" was published in *Putnam's Magazine* in July 1854. On the assumption that Tuckerman would have included the third series of sonnets in the 1860 volume had they been complete, it appears that they were written between 1860 and 1872. By the same logic the unpublished poems and *The Cricket* fall into this period also. The notebook which contains sonnet series three, four, and five is dated 1872. The narrative arrangement of some of the later sonnets provides evidence that they were written in the order in which they are numbered and preserved.

As indicated in the description of manuscripts, Appendix II, *The Cricket* exists in four copies in Tuckerman's hand. I believe the copies to have been written in the order suggested in Appendix III.

APPENDIX II

*

MANUSCRIPTS, EDITIONS, AND PUBLICATIONS

THE TUCKERMAN MANUSCRIPTS are preserved in the Houghton Library at Harvard University. They were given to the Houghton Library by Mr. Orton Loring Clark, whose late wife was Margaret Tuckerman, the poet's granddaughter. Altogether the manuscript items number eleven, not including the autograph file, which contains several letters. The Tuckerman manuscripts are catalogued under the citation MS Am 1349. A description of manuscript items follows.

1. Notebook; "To Frederick Goddard Tuckerman from Santa Claus, Dec. 25, 1830."; pencil drawings in a child's hand and several disconnected words and sentences.

2. Notebook; "F. G. Tuckerman, Litchfield Eng. 1854" and "Poems by Frederick G Tuckerman"; the *Poems* in ink with pencil corrections and notations.

3. Notebook; "F G Tuckerman"; pencil (predominantly) and ink drafts of numerous poems, including *The Cricket*.

4. Notebook; *The Cricket*; "G. D. W."; "The Shore"; "An Incident"; "Ode for the Greenfield Soldiers Monument"; "Lines Written in the Blue Ridge, Virginia"; and "Under the Locust Blossoms."

5. Notebook; "F G Tuckerman Greenfield Dec 1872."; sonnet series third, fourth, and fifth in ink.

6. Notebook; "F G Tuckerman."; ink (predominantly) and pencil sonnet series first and second.

7. Portfolio:

j. Letter fragment including lines from "Poesy." The poem, "Poesy," if it was completed, has not come down to us, and the person to whom the letter was addressed is not named. The fragment reads as follows:

I have endeavoured to retouch these lines, as I do not believe I can recast them in better shape—and do not want to waste the stuff.

> Thou art not fled—
> Stunned by the din of this mechanic age;
> Nor chilled by wayward stress,
> Of wind and cloud to silentness;
> Nor in a poet's hermitage,
> Hidest thy gleaning head;
> Though still unwooed thy form the sight evades;
> But here amid our glens and dark blue scenery,
> And rivulets frilled with fern, and soft cascades,
> Rustling down steps of sandstone ceaselessly,
> And rocks and banks of pines,
> Thy solemn beauty wanes and shines;
> Have I not seen thee in the river glades?
> Or from a mountain gallery leaning down,
> Mid depths of green behold thy starlike crown,
> And vaguely caught the wonder of thy song?
> While crag and stream and foliaged throng,
> Glittered as tinted by the morning's wand;

The first six lines I have not touched, the 7th is perhaps an improvement,—8th—'dark blue scenery' I cannot improve, 'cascades' I do not like very well but I suppose may be allowed for rhyme's sake at least, 'Rustling' you disapprove of (10th). I retain this word because in the first place it suggested itself naturally, when listening to the 'soft cascade,' secondly because I find upon examination that Mr. Emerson has observed it,

> "By Fate, not option frugal nature gave,
> One sound to pine grove and to waterfall,"

and thirdly because I discovered the other day in an old ballad, [title undecipherable], a beautiful use made of this identical expression.

> 'The monster slept on an island crag
> Lulled by the rustling chear
> Which eddied turbid at the base,
> Tho elsewhere smooth and clear.'

There I think I have beaten you on that—same line 'ceaselessly' I must have an adverb here and cannot find a better one—without 'restlessly' or 'tremulously' may do. Your objection that the current *cannot* always flow I do not think fair. 'I watched—and the great River the streamlet's ceaseless flow over its rocks ceaselessly bursts and raves' Shelley. I suppose the writer means while he is looking at them, or listening (11th) 'banks of pines'—I mean by this not only 'piny banks' but real banks as they appear in the distance—"Like the sweet South, Which breathes upon a bank of violets." And Ossian talks about 'hills of grass'—'upland throng,' line 17th I have changed, but why is the original expression more obscure than 'mountain throng' which is in common use. I do not understand your objection to the 20th and 21st lines as it originally stood—
"When the fair West with breathings overpowers"—
is it "From orchards blanched with bloom"—because overpowers is an active verb? Then may not the substantive be understood? Or may it not be used as a neuter verb, as is often done in poetry—as, the picture pleases—'ripe with flowers,' I have altered,—23rd line 'Tanned with the fallen fibres'—you do not like. I can only say that it seems to me new and expressive. Some poet I forget who, Shakespeare I think, speaks of the pines as 'waving their fibrous tops.' Mr. Emerson calls the leaves 'strings' and Longfellow speaks of the 'carpet of golden threads,' and I think in all humility mine as good as either. 26th line is designed to be shorter by one syllable than the succeeding. 27, the verb here is 'sitting' not 'flitting.' The [undecipherable] part of the remainder I mean to re-write, but do you think the above is improved, or worthy of being preserved from the burning

k. "An Incident"

l. "An Incident"

8. Notebook; "Journal Astronomical & Meteorological for 1847 Greenfield."; daily observations of weather and astronomical phenomena for the years 1848, 1849, and 1850.

9. Scrapbook; newspaper reviews of *Poems* and a name-list of those to whom that volume was given.

10. Scrapbook; poems, chiefly by Tennyson, obituaries clipped from newspapers, and poems transcribed in Tuckerman's hand.

11. Herbarium; "Wild Flowers—gathered in Scotland and Eng during the summer of 1851 Greenfield Sept 1st 51–".

The editions of the *Poems* contain minute variations. The book was first printed in 1860 by John Wilson and Son, 22 School Street, Boston. The second edition was published by Smith, Elder and Company of London in 1863. Between these editions the differences are as follows: in "The School Girl: an Idyll", lines 69, 70, and 71 read as follows:

> And told an Indian story of the place,—
> Of Wassahoale and Phoebe Bellflower,—
> Until her face grew clear again and calm,

In the 1863 edition, these lines were altered as follows:

> And told an Indian story of the place,—
> Of Wassahoale and the fair Quaker maid,
> Who left the log-hut for a chieftain's lodge,
> Until her face grew clear again and calm,

The final lines of "Sidney", in the edition of 1860, reads as follows:

> Sweet as yourself, and of one lustre too;
> Not York and Lancaster, nor white nor yellow,
> But a rose-coloured rose.

But the 1863 edition reads

> Sweet as yourself, and of one lustre too;
> Let not the red dark bud Damascus yields,
> Nor York-and-Lancaster, nor white, nor yellow,
> But a rose-coloured rose.

In 1864 Ticknor and Fields issued the *Poems* in Boston. The type for the table of contents was re-set, but the plates of the 1863 edition were used for the text, and the poems are therefore identical, as are the lists of errata. In 1869, Little, Brown, and Company issued its printing of the *Poems*, again making use of the Smith, Elder plates. The Little, Brown issue did not contain a list of errata. All editions and impressions of the *Poems* are long since out of print.

In 1931 Witter Bynner's edition of Tuckerman's sonnets was published by Alfred A. Knopf and Company. That edition is also out of print.

In 1950 *The Cricket* was published by the Cummington Press, then of Cummington, Massachusetts. The Cummington edition was based on a faulty version of the poem in manuscript, and it contains several errors which were acknowledged and corrected in a list of errata. In 1960, Mordecai Marcus published *The Cricket* in the autumn issue of *The Massachusetts Review*.

The poem "May Flowers" appeared in *Littell's Living Age*, October 19, 1850. "Picomegan" was published in *Putnam's Magazine*, July 1854. "Rhotruda," the sonnet "The starry flower," and "Coralie" were published in *The Atlantic Monthly*, July 1861, June 1862, and April 1863, respectively.

APPENDIX III

*

TUCKERMAN'S *Cricket*: THE VERSIONS

HERETOFORE, *The Cricket* has not been published in its correct form. There have been only two published versions of the complete poem, and neither is based upon the best version in manuscript. *The Cricket* was published for the first time by the editors of the Cummington Press in 1950, more than seventy years after the poet's death. In the same year, Yvor Winters published a critique of *The Cricket* which appeared in *The Hudson Review* (Autumn 1950), and in which about a third of the poem was transcribed. The transcription was of course based upon the Cummington Press edition.

In 1952, Samuel A. Golden published a monograph under the title, *Frederick Goddard Tuckerman: An American Sonneteer*, in the University of Maine Studies series. Golden's monograph has been the only attempt to deal with Tuckerman's life and the entire corpus of his poems; it is especially valuable as biography, and it contains a useful bibliography. Golden evidently examined the Tuckerman manuscripts with care. A section of his study is given to a discussion of the unpublished poems, wherein he includes *The Cricket*. He had seen Yvor Winters's review, and he thought it exaggerated. Of the unpublished poems, Golden elected to present only those, or parts thereof, which he regarded with favor. Presumably he had access to the complete manuscripts, yet his quotations from *The Cricket* are drawn, as he says, from the Cummington Press edition.

In the autumn of 1960, Mordecai Marcus published *The Cricket,*

[209]

with a brief introductory note, in *The Massachusetts Review*. The Marcus version is a distinct improvement upon the Cummington Press edition. It is, however, faulty in several details.

There are in the Tuckerman manuscripts four versions of the poem, which I shall call *Crickets 1, 2, 3,* and *4,* after the order in which they appear and in which I believe they were written. *Cricket 1* is more truly a draft than are the others. Part III of *Cricket 1* precedes by a page Parts I, II, IV, and V, which are otherwise entered in correct order under the title. The punctuation is largely defective, certain lines are altered, and there are one or two minor aspects of structure which are to be found in this version only.

Cricket 1 seems to be the basis of the Cummington Press edition. In both versions line 50 reads as follows:

Thou bringest too, lost accents from the grave

But in *Crickets 2, 3,* and *4* the word "dim" has been substituted for the word "lost." In line 59, the Cummington Press edition follows *Cricket 1* in printing the word "twilights"; the proper form is obviously possessive, and the word is correctly written with an apostrophe in the other manuscript versions. Line 81 of both the Cummington Press edition and *Cricket 1* reads as follows:

Though all the forest wailed to horns of Arcady?

But *Crickets 2, 3,* and *4* contain a somewhat different line,

Though the lost forest wailed to horns of Arcady?

although the line in *Cricket 3* ends with a period rather than a question mark. Finally, lines 21 and 117 of both versions are indented. In the other manuscript versions these lines are set back to the margin. The list of errata in the Cummington Press edition indicates that other versions of the poem were seen after the setting of the type. At any rate, *Cricket 1* appears to have been the sole model for the text of the Cummington Press edition.

I believe *Cricket 2* to have been written soon after *Cricket 1*. It has the appearance of a finished performance. In general the punctuation is improved, but it remains in need of further improvement. Several words have been changed; notably, "faltering" has replaced "falling" in line 25, "dim" has replaced "lost" in line 50, "morning" has replaced "happy" in line 55, "closing" has taken the place of "final" in line 58, "shimmering" has replaced "glimmering" in line 68, the word "dusky" has been inserted before "rainbow" in line 107, and "windward" has replaced "windy" in line 110. Not all of these changes are for the better, and, fortunately, Tuckerman did not retain them all in the last and best version. Notwithstanding, it seems highly probable that *Cricket 2* follows directly *Cricket 1* in point of time and represents an effort to improve upon a tentative rendition.

Crickets 3 and *4* exist as separate pieces in the manuscripts. *Cricket 3*, like *Cricket 1*, appears to be a draft. Line 35 of the other versions has been omitted. Lines 106 and 110 (lines 105 and 109 of *Cricket 3*) are not included in the body of the poem, but are written perpendicular to the other lines in the left margin. Beginning with line 108 (line 107 of *Cricket 3*), the remainder of the poem was written with a pencil instead of a pen—possibly at a later date. Curiously, *Cricket 3* is almost entirely unpunctuated. Where punctuation exists at all, it is limited, with but five exceptions, to the interior of a few lines. With only one exception, there are no words in *Cricket 3* which are not also contained in one or more of the other versions: in line 50 (line 49 of *Cricket 3*), the word "accents" Tuckerman changed to "voices."

If *Cricket 3* is indeed a draft, as I believe it to be, it is nonetheless superior to *Cricket 2*, especially in its diction. I would venture the speculation that Tuckerman, sometime after the composition of *Crickets 1* and *2*, set down *Cricket 3*, without punctuation, as a necessary and preparatory step to the writing of *Cricket 4*. He might well have been dissatisfied with his punctuation of the two earlier versions. *Cricket 3* served a most useful purpose: it provided Tuckerman with a *Cricket* stripped to its essentials, a kind of skeleton poem, unobscured by the myriad and often faulty punctuation of the earlier models. It was, I think, an intelligent and successful effort to see the forest by removing the near trees.

The authority for Mordecai Marcus's version of the poem appears to have been a combination of three versions only: *Crickets*

1 and *2*, and the Cummington Press edition. Marcus, in his introductory note, states that he took his version literally from a draft in Tuckerman's notebook. That statement would seem to preclude the possibility that Marcus saw, or made use of, *Crickets 3* and *4*; as previously noted, these versions are not contained in notebooks. Moreover, Marcus's version is identical with either *Cricket 1* or *2* in instances too numerous to mention. The punctuation adheres closely to these versions, and it is quite unlike that of *Cricket 4*. Like *Cricket 1* and the Cummington Press edition, the Marcus version indents line 21; this is not the case in *Crickets 2, 3,* and *4*. Marcus's word "dim" in line 50 does not occur in *Cricket 1* or the Cummington Press edition, but it occurs in *Cricket 2* as well as *3* and *4*. His word "shimmering" in line 68 occurs in *Crickets 2* and *3* only. The word "dusky" in line 107 occurs in Marcus and *Crickets 2* and *3*. Line 117 is indented in Marcus, *Cricket 1,* and the Cummington Press edition only. In brief, there seems to be no evidence that Marcus was aware of the best version in manuscript, *Cricket 4*; indeed, the perceptibly superior character of *Cricket 4* seems itself to be the best evidence that he was not.

Another fact indicates that Marcus is mistaken in his assertion that he transcribed "literally" from the manuscripts. Line 68 of his version reads as follows:

And perfect tears, and crowning vacancy!

It is true that Tuckerman was uncertain with respect to the second word in this line. In the margin of *Cricket 1,* and roughly opposite the line, he wrote the two words "perfect" and "closing." The word "final" seems surely to be the choice he ultimately settled upon; it appears in three of the versions, including *Cricket 4*. Only in *Cricket 2* did he substitute another word into the text, and there the word is "closing." The editor of the Cummington Press edition was the first to bring "perfect" into the text, though he brought it in by way of the list of errata. I would agree with both editors that "perfect" is .a better word than either of the others which Tuckerman considered alternative, and I have included the word in the present text. The fact remains, however, that "perfect" does not occur in the text of any one of the manuscript versions.

INDEX OF FIRST LINES

But grief finds solace faint in others' ills   20
But into order falls our life at last,   45
But man finds means, grant him but place and room,   60
But Nature in her mood pushes or pulls   41
But Nature where she gives must give in kind,   59
But the heart murmurs at so harsh a tone.   32
But Thought, like a mailed archer helmed and tall,   51
But unto him came swift calamity   23
But war his overturning trumpet blew.   54
But we are set to strive to make our mark   48
By this low fire I often sit to woo   15

Companions were we in the grove and glen,   22

Dank fens of cedar, hemlock branches gray   6

Each common object too, the house, the grove,   30
Ere the first red-orange glimmer   116
Even as a lover, dreaming, unaware,   25

Farewell, farewell, O noble heart! I dreamed   36
For Nature daily through her grand design   15
For these, my friend, were but the foldings fair,   63

Gertrude and Gulielma, sister-twins,   26
Gunhilda, lady of my love and theme,   187

Hast thou seen reversed the prophet's miracle—   55
Have you forgotten that still afternoon?   156
Her beauty came to his distrustful heart   96
Here, where the red man swept the leaves away   55
Here, where the River wheels   97
His heart was in his garden; but his brain   22
How most unworthy, echoing in mine ears,   24
How oft in schoolboy-days, from the school's sway   33
How shall I array my love?   89
How strange a paradox is human life,   87
How well do I recall that walk in state   43

[216]